*the mo

essentials

amanda statham

foulsham
LONDON • NEW YORK • TORONTO • SYDNEY

foulsham

The Publishing House, Bennetts Close, Cippenham,
Slough, Berkshire, SL1 5AP, England

ISBN 0-572-02870-9

Printed in Great Britain by Cox & Wyman Ltd, Reading, Berkshire

Contents

Introduction

Congratulations! He's popped the question (or maybe you did) and now you're all set to prepare for one of the biggest, and happiest, days of your life.

There's never been a better time to be a bride, because there are so many choices available today that you're bound to find something to suit your style, from a modern city 'do' to a traditional white wedding.

Wherever you choose to say 'I do', as the bride you'll be the star of the day, which is both thrilling and daunting. You'll also be the key organiser, which is why it's essential that you have plenty of helpers, so get your mum, friends, relatives and your groom on board with the wedding plans as soon as possible.

You'll also have this book, which will become your new best friend as it's packed full of planning tips and wedding-day ideas to make sure that you have the smoothest run-up to a wedding day ever. It covers all of the important aspects you need to consider in order to ensure a blissful day, from choosing the right dress to making sure that the invitations and thank-you cards go out on time.

It's also crammed with style and beauty tips, because we know you're going to want to look a million dollars on the day. And there's practical advice for the modern bride on how to go about booking the church and getting the licence, and whether or not to change your name.

Most couples' biggest wedding worry is a financial one, and with the average UK wedding costing £13,500, it's no wonder. That's why we've dedicated a whole chapter to helping you draw up a budget plan – and sticking to it. In each chapter we suggest lots of ways to save money and still make your wedding look spectacular, so that you can chill out and concentrate on the important issues like finding the perfect wedding cake and shoes!

Throughout you'll find handy hints and tips to make the build-up to your wedding day less stressful, and at the back of the book you'll find the contact details for hundreds of wedding-day suppliers who are the best in the business.

Slip it into your handbag and dip in when ever you need a helping hand, whether it's choosing your bouquet or applying your make-up. We guarantee you'll look and feel sensational – just don't forget to keep your man included in all of the preparations!

Enjoy!

Chapter 1
Getting Started

Planning a wedding is incredibly exciting. Who hasn't daydreamed about what they'd wear to walk up the aisle or how they'd design their perfect cake?

To some, however, planning the dream day is also a rather daunting task. Juggling a job and home can be hard enough without having to arrange the wedding of the year, so this chapter is designed to help you make it as fun and easy as possible, no matter what your circumstances. You may have already discussed some of the issues, but there are bound to be some areas that you are unsure of, so we aim to cover everything that a recently engaged couple could want to know.

The engagement

You don't need to get engaged to get married, but lots of couples like their family and friends to know that they've made a serious commitment and to use the engagement time – anything from a month to a couple of years – to plan the wedding and get used to the idea of becoming Mr and Mrs.

Should we have an engagement party?

It may once have been *de rigeur* to have a big party, but modern brides do as they please. You may be happy simply to telephone family and friends with the good news, however, a party is a good way to kick off the celebrations and an ideal chance for pals that haven't met before to get to know each other before your wedding day. For an informal gathering, invite people round to your house or your parents' house for drinks. Or you could get together for a meal at a restaurant or hotel. If you want your engagement to have maximum impact, you could always hold a party and then make the announcement a surprise during the evening. Whatever you decide to do, crack open the champagne because a celebratory toast will really get you in the wedding spirit.

Do we announce our engagement officially?

For some couples a phone call, e-mail or letter is enough to let family and friends know that they've decided to take the plunge. Others like to announce it officially in a local or national newspaper, or their parents may ask if they could put it in. If you're going down the public route the announcement should read something like the following:

> Mr NJ Collins and Miss Emma Smith
> The engagement is announced between Nicholas John Collins, youngest son of Mr and Mrs Alfred Collins of Birstall, Leicestershire, and Miss Emma Smith, youngest daughter of Mr and Mrs Robert Smith of Hereford.

Check how much the announcement will cost and to avoid any errors going into the paper don't send a handwritten note; type it and then fax or e-mail it to the publication. If the announcement is noted down by someone over the phone, spell out each word.

Choosing an engagement ring

He may well have got down and proposed on bended knee and presented you with a perfect ring. If so, congratulations, and move on to the next section. Chances are, however, he wasn't quite sure if his choice would be your taste and waited until you could buy the ring together. Or he may have simply proposed on the spur of the moment and didn't have time to shop for a ring.

Either way, you'll want to go shopping for a rock as soon as you can, finances permitting! Tradition dictates that the groom buys the engagement and wedding rings and spends around a month's salary on them, but lots of couples club together to buy their ideal rings.

It's best to spend a romantic day or two shopping around for your ring before you make a decision. Try on lots of different styles; remember, you're going to be wearing this for the rest of your life so think about what's going to look good 30 years from now.

The classic engagement ring is a diamond solitaire because the cut and stone make it fantastically sparkly, and it's also hard wearing and symbolises love and eternity. If you're not the kind of girl who does diamonds, consider other precious gems such as rubies, emeralds and sapphires. Think about the metal you want your stone set in; gold is traditional but platinum is currently in vogue and is the least likely to wear away of any of the expensive metals.

One of the most important things to remember is that your ring will sit next to your wedding band, so they should complement each other. Lots of jewellers make matching wedding and engagement rings, so be sure to ask to look at sets.

How soon should we set the date?

As soon as possible! The first thing the two of you have to do, after telling your relatives and friends that you're engaged, is to decide when you're going to get married. You can then look for and book a venue, and let family and friends know so that they can keep that date free in their diaries. It also gives you a deadline to work to.

When setting your date, there are several things to consider:

- Be realistic about how soon you're going to be able to get married. Remember that most venues, caterers, guests, dress designers and florists are going to need from six to twelve months' warning.
- Are your family and close friends going to be available?
- Do you want to go out-of-season and cut costs?
- Where do you want to go on honeymoon? Some long-haul destinations have better weather during the UK's winter months.

The serious stuff

Arranging your wedding can be great fun, but that doesn't mean the act of marriage itself should be taken lightly. This is a life-changing day you're building up to, and there are some issues that you need to look at before you can throw yourself into the wedding preparations.

Can I marry anyone?

No! But as long as you're both of sound mind and acting by your own consent, are not closely related, already married or going through a divorce, and are aged 16 or over you're free to wed. If you are under 18 you must have your parents' or legal guardians' consent.

What's my role?

You are the star of the show, so the wedding is going to take shape around your ideas. You have all of the fun parts of the wedding preparations, like shopping for your dress and accessories, but don't forget it's your partner's day too, so don't leave him out of any of the important decisions like choosing the cake or venue.

Although lots of couples now share the decisions, traditionally your duties include coming up with the theme of the wedding and deciding on the details like stationery, the cake and flowers. You usually choose the chief bridesmaid and attendants, and have a say in the venue.

The groom's job is to organise the legal side of the marriage, such as getting the licence, paying the ceremony fees and completing any necessary paperwork. Other vital requirements, apart from saying 'I do', are choosing the best man, buying the wedding rings, buying presents for the attendants, hiring the wedding transport and making a speech at the reception.

Should I change my name?

This is entirely up to you, as you don't legally have to take your husband's family name. Lots of women do decide to make the swap to symbolise their union; for other women who want to retain their surname it's a definite no.

If you're divided on this issue, there are compromises. You could always link your two last names with or without a hyphen, or create a new last name that combines the two. Another option is to use your husband's name socially, but to keep your own name for work. This is particularly relevant if you are well known in your chosen profession and a name change could be detrimental.

Whichever course of action you choose, the important thing is to arrange for the relevant authorities to update your identity. Your marriage certificate will be one of your primary documents of identification, so it's a good idea to get multiple copies made. You're then prepared in case you need to post a copy with an application for a name change.

The two major items to change are your passport and driving licence. You will have to request a new passport by post, or you could call in to a passport office. Remember that you must do this several months before your wedding if you are planning a honeymoon overseas. Also vital are changes to your bank and credit card accounts, and mortgage and insurance policies.

How can we prevent any disasters?

The key to avoiding problems is good planning. Think about what could go wrong and do all you can to prevent it happening. It's better to have thought the worst beforehand than to be fazed on the big day. Things that can go wrong include bad weather, a key member of your wedding party being unable to make it at the last minute or a major supplier not meeting the deadline.

Have a list of contact numbers for people or companies that may be able to help out at the last minute. Keep in contact with all of your suppliers to check on progress and make sure they know exactly when the wedding date is, particularly if you booked them months in advance.

☺ Keep all paperwork from your wedding suppliers together in a safe place, so you can access it straight away.

Learn to delegate

Unless you're superwoman, it's unlikely that you're going to be able to handle all of the wedding preparations on your own, particularly if you're working full-time. You're going to have to learn to delegate and trust other members of the wedding party to take on some responsibility.

If you have a good relationship with your mum or perhaps the groom's mother, then don't be afraid to ask for assistance; they're sure to be delighted and flattered that you asked. Your chief bridesmaid should also be a rock who will help you through any crisis. There are lots of small jobs, such as addressing invitations and monitoring the gift list, that they could help with. It's not a military operation, but it's a good idea to draw up a schedule early on of who you want to do what. Also include any dates and times when they have to be available for fittings, rehearsals and so on.

Ask everyone involved to come round to your house for a drink and to discuss their role and their major requirements. Most of all, remember that it's teamwork that makes a wedding successful, so keep in touch regularly. Ask for everyone's e-mail addresses and send regular updates. It won't take more than a couple of minutes, but it's a great way of making everyone feel involved and aware of what stage you're at in your preparations.

☺ Buy a year planner to put on the wall – that way you can check your appointments at a glance.

Deciding on your wedding style

After you've set the date and chosen your wedding party, you can start the exciting task of choosing the type of wedding you both want. Do you want to have a small, intimate affair or to fill a cathedral with 500 people? Will your ceremony be civil or religious? (See Chapter 3.)

What are the choices?

There's no limit on how large and grand or small and intimate your wedding can be. Some couples have a set idea early on of the type of wedding they want, but many people don't, and need inspiration for their dream wedding. A great place to start if you fall into the latter category is with weddings you have been to. If you've been a guest at a wedding that you felt was particularly charming then think what it was about that occasion that made it so special. Alternatively, if you have been to a wedding that you felt wasn't ideal, then you'll know that won't be the route you'll be taking for your own big day.

Further inspiration can be gathered from your lives together: do you share a hobby or interest that could be used as a theme for the day? Remember, there are very few places these days where you can't get married, so if you both have, for example, a passion for deep-sea diving, why not get married under the water?

Further inspiration can be taken from the time of year you choose to hold your wedding. If you are having a winter wedding, you could theme it around the season and opt for a country house with roaring fires, candles and decorations made of holly, and serve up punch drinks. Similarly, an autumn wedding could be centred around autumnal colours like orange, brown and deep reds.

Wedding magazines are also a good source of inspiration when you're at the early stages of planning the theme of your wedding. Particularly useful are articles on real-life weddings, as they demonstrate not only how different weddings can be, but also the fact that you don't have to stick to the tried-and-tested formula of a church wedding followed by a marquee reception – there are lots more options out there if that's not your cup of tea.

Wedding traditions and superstitions

Wow your mother-in-law with this quick low-down on wedding traditions, and prove that you may be a modern bride who knows her Manolo Blahniks from her Jimmy Choos, but you also know the meaning behind the exchanging of rings and throwing your bouquet!

The most symbolic tradition during the wedding is the exchange of rings. The circle represents never-ending love and faithfulness, while the metal symbolises constant love. It's placed on the third finger of the left hand because it was believed that a vein in this finger is connected directly with the heart.

Some brides carry silver horseshoes in their bouquet or use them as decorations because they are a symbol of good luck, fertility and vitality. They should always be pointing upwards, however, as the luck drains away if they point down.

Bouquets are carried by the bride to ward off evil spirits. They were originally made up of herbs rather than flowers.

You may well have heard the familiar saying 'something old, something new, something borrowed, something blue, and a lucky sixpence in your shoe'. 'Something old, something new' represents passing from your old life to your new one with your husband.

'Something borrowed' symbolises that marriage is about sharing, while 'something blue' refers to the colour's association with constancy – so why not include some lavender in your bouquet, or have it tied with blue ribbon?

Some brides wear a garter on their wedding day. In ancient times it represented a virginal girdle, so when the groom removed it, it symbolised the bride's relinquishing of her virginity!

When the bride is ready to leave the house, it is thought to be good luck to look in the mirror once just before departing. Returning to the mirror, however, is meant to be bad luck. We don't think a quick peek in a powder compact to check your make-up on the way to the church will do any harm though!

Your wedding is a great occasion for singles who are looking for their own Mr Right. According to wedding traditions, if unmarried guests place a piece of wedding cake under their pillow before sleeping it will increase their prospects of finding a partner, while bridesmaids will dream of their future husband. An unmarried friend who catches your bouquet (thrown over your shoulder) will be the next to marry.

Bridesmaids were traditionally dressed in similar outfits to the bride to confuse evil spirits by acting as decoys and protecting the bride.

There are supposedly lots of good luck symbols to be spotted on the way to your wedding, including chimney sweeps, rainbows, black cats and lambs. And don't get upset if it unexpectedly snows on your wedding day, as it represents fertility and wealth.

Choosing the bridal party

Choosing the bridal party early is essential to enable everyone to keep the date free in their diary, and so that they can play a big part in helping with the planning and organisation. For some couples, choosing the bridal party can be a daunting prospect. You don't want to offend anyone, or leave anyone out, but how many people can you realistically include?

Should I have bridesmaids?

The tradition of having wedding attendants descends from ancient Greece, when a girl got married surrounded by married women because it was thought to bring her good luck. In the UK attendants dressed to look like the bride to fool evil spirits. While you may not need them to ward off spirits, apart from, perhaps, your mad old Aunt Ethel, having your girlfriends supporting you on the day is a tremendous feeling and certainly adds to the fun.

The most important role, apart from the best man, whom the groom usually chooses, is that of the maid (or matron if she's married) of honour. Traditionally the bride's sister closest to her in age takes the role; if there are two sisters and one doesn't want to be left out, they could share the title. However, it's perfectly acceptable for brides to ask anyone to whom they are close to take up the role.

It's got to be someone that you can rely on and trust, and who won't let you down. You may have some friends who are a great laugh when you're on a night out, but who could not necessarily be relied upon to turn up at fittings on time or patiently help you try on 150 identical wedding shoes. On the day, she'll be there to help you dress, to hold your bouquet during the ceremony and to act as one of the witnesses.

The other bridesmaids and ushers are usually made up of family and friends, such as the groom's sister as bridesmaid or the bride's brother as an usher, but again this depends on your circumstances. There's no right or wrong number of attendants, although the size of the wedding normally dictates. As a guideline, it's usual to have one attendant and one usher for every 50 guests, but it's up to you.

If you've got some younger relatives, you might want to involve them as bridesmaids or pageboys. Do think about how long they will be expected to stand around for and don't give them tasks that are too onerous. Careful thought will also be needed when it comes to their clothing. You may even choose to have a flower girl. Usually the smallest of the bridesmaids, she walks in front of the happy couple, throwing petals in their path.

How do we keep everyone happy?

Remember that this is a big responsibility that you're asking people to take on, so while they may be flattered to have been asked, don't be hurt if they decline. You should ask people in a way that allows them to feel comfortable with turning down your request. Your letter could be worded: 'It would be an honour if you would be one of my bridesmaids, but if you can't take on the role, please let me know.' Some people won't want the spotlight to be on them, and would prefer to help out in some other way, such as helping with the catering.

On the other hand, remember that feelings can run high when it comes to weddings, and you may well discover that someone is hurt that you didn't ask them to play a lead role. If this happens, don't let bad feeling simmer away, talk to them about it and ask them to play another important part on the day, such as giving a reading.

Help! I need a professional

For some people the task of organising a wedding is not a daunting task, it is impossible! Time may simply not be available for you to do all of the necessary preparations for your wedding day. In some circumstances the stress of the preparations may even be detrimental to your relationship. In cases like these, some couples opt to employ a professional wedding co-ordinator.

A good wedding planner will help you to decide the theme of your wedding, help organise all of the details like flowers and photography, and make sure that everything runs smoothly on the day.

It is highly recommended that you see several wedding co-ordinators before you make your final decision, as this will allow you to compare and contrast the services on offer. It is very important that you meet the person who will be dealing specifically with your wedding, as you will be seeing a lot of this person and it is vital that you get on.

It is also essential to find out what experience the planner has at organising weddings, and to see examples of previous work. A good wedding planner should be able to provide references.

The downside of employing an expert to organise your wedding is the cost – a good wedding planner can charge thousands of pounds, so you've got to be absolutely certain before taking the plunge.

If you decide to go ahead with external help, do make sure that you are aware of the exact content of any contract to which you are agreeing. Watch out for hidden charges, and ask for a detailed list of what is included in the service, and what is not.

Hen nights

Okay, so there's lots of hectic planning to be done to prepare for the big day, but this doesn't mean you shouldn't give a little thought to potentially one of the most fun nights (or weekends) of your life!

When do I have my hen night?

Hen nights usually take place a week or two before the big day. It's a bad idea to have hen or stag nights the night before the wedding, mainly because you aren't going to enjoy or remember much of your first day of married life together if you've got a terrible hangover!

Whether you want the party to end all parties or a quiet night in watching videos with your best pals, your wedding is a perfect excuse to have a night celebrating with the girls. You may want it to coincide with your fiancé's stag night, so that you can go out separately with your friends and then meet up at the end of the night. Most women, however, choose to keep the two parties separate.

What's an ideal hen night?

A popular choice is a meal followed by a pub crawl or night club. You could always try something new and unusual like salsa dancing, which gets everyone involved. Active brides with active friends may want to make a day of it and have a go at white-water rafting, go-kart racing or paint balling, followed by drinks.

If a cosy night in gossiping is more appealing, why not invite your friends to the ultimate slumber party. Try out beauty products, rent some classic videos like *Pretty Woman* and *Dirty Dancing*, and each bring some finger food, like sushi, pop corn or tortilla chips and dips.

The ultimate hen party is a trip abroad. Popular destinations include Dublin, Amsterdam and Barcelona. Budget airlines have made popping overseas for a weekend break much more affordable, and leave you with plenty of spending money for drinks, food and shopping. Some brides go one step further and make their hen party a holiday, staying away for a week or more. If this appeals to you, you'll have to give friends a lot of advance warning so that they can budget for it, and be aware that some pals may not be able to come because of the price. Popular week-long hen hot spots are Ibiza and New York.

> ☺ Book a date as early as possible to give friends plenty of warning and get it booked in their diaries.

Wedding countdown

The sooner you get going on the wedding plans the better. Ideally, you should allow six months to make sure you're going to get the caterer, florist, cake designer and venue that you want, but as engagements become shorter, this isn't always possible. Below is a comprehensive planner that covers everything you will find in more detail in the book and is designed to get you on track straight away. It shows at a glance what needs to be done when, but if your time frame is shorter, don't panic. Personalise it with your own wedding deadlines and get planning!

As soon as possible
❏ Announce your engagement in the local papers: This is the best, and easiest, way to announce to everyone that you're getting married. It's also a great keepsake.

29|30 July 06

❑ **Pick a wedding date:** Remember, a lot of venues and churches are booked up to a year in advance, particularly on Saturdays, so have some back-up dates in mind and be prepared to be flexible.

❑ **Decide what type of wedding you want:** This is a big decision as it's going to set the tone of the whole day, so take your time and look around for inspiration.

❑ **Set your budget:** Do this as soon as you can – and stick to it!

❑ **Choose your ceremony venue and reserve it for the big day:** The best venues get booked up very early on.

❑ **Determine what, if any, religion the service will be performed in:** This is between you and your groom to decide. (Read about your choices in Chapter 3.)

❑ **Choose your reception venue and reserve it:** When choosing, it's a good idea to have a couple of reserve places in mind in case your first choice is already booked.

❑ **Choose and book your photographer/videographer:** Get going and book yours as soon as you can so you get the one you want.

❑ **Choose your bridesmaids:** You need to do this well in advance so that they can keep the wedding date free.

❑ **Choose and hire your florist and cake maker:** These two people will play a vital part in your wedding day, so make appointments to see their work as soon as possible. You'll need to allow them plenty of time to work on your wedding-day designs.

❑ **Decide what type of music your want for the ceremony and reception:** Start listening to lots of CDs and making appointments with bands or orchestras.

❑ **Book musicians for the ceremony and reception:** When you've found the right group, book them straight away!

❑ **Choose the reception format (sit-down, buffet or canapés):** This will largely depend on your venue and budget.

❑ **Choose and hire your caterer:** If they aren't in-house at your reception venue, you'll need to hire caterers. Remember to sample their food before you go ahead.

❑ **Choose your wedding dress:** Be sure to try on lots of different styles to ensure that the dress perfectly complements your body shape.

Six months to go

❑ **Decide if all or part of the vows will be written by you and your groom:** For a civil ceremony, it's a great touch to personalise it with your own vows. A religious ceremony is less flexible.

❑ **Reserve any rental items such as chairs, tables and glassware:** You'll need these if your venue or caterer does not hire items.

❑ **Meet with the minister/officiant:** Be prepared to be asked to attend church services in the run-up to your wedding if you're having a church ceremony.

❑ **Decide the size of the wedding party:** Match it to the size of your venue. If you want to have extra friends attending but can't afford it, why not invite them to the evening reception?

❑ **Make a first draft of the invitation list:** Start with close family first, then other relatives, friends and work colleagues.

❑ **Choose your gift-list company:** Have a good look round stores where you fancy having a gift list, and check out things like how helpful the staff are and whether they have a good stock of products.

❑ **Hire your transport:** Your groom should be in charge of this area, but there's nothing to stop you getting involved. Think about the dress you'll be wearing before booking a tiny sports car!

❏ **Decide what type of wedding cake and filling you will have and order it:** Have a yummy afternoon at your cake maker's, tasting delicious pieces of cake of all varieties before you finally plump for one.

❏ **Choose the stationery:** This includes invites, orders of service, menus, place cards and thank-you cards.

❏ **Purchase your wedding rings:** Give yourself lots of time to visit jewellers and find the perfect rings. Or you could have them commissioned.

❏ **Choose your wedding shoes:** Remember, you'll be on your feet all day, so they've got to be comfortable as well as look fantastic.

❏ **Choose other wedding accessories such as gloves, a bag or a tiara:** If possible, try them on with your dress.

❏ **Choose or start making your favours:** These small gifts for wedding guests require some thought, so start thinking about them in advance. Either decide on having them made or, if you're doing the work yourself, enlist a friend to help you.

❏ **Reserve accommodation for any out-of-town guests:** Or you could send them details of local hotels and B&Bs.

❏ **Help pick out the groom's, best man's and ushers' outfits:** Let him know what colour scheme you're going for in your bouquet and other details, so that he'll know what to choose and what to avoid.

❏ **Choose outfits for the bridesmaids:** Don't feel you have to be restricted to specialist bridesmaid labels – go shopping on the high street for chic, modern gowns.

❏ **Check that the groom is booking the honeymoon:** If you're not choosing this together, give him some subtle hints.

❏ **Check passports and visas:** Check their expiry dates and send off for a new passport if you are changing your name after the wedding.

❏ **Begin writing vows and choosing readings, if necessary:** There are lots of books on the subject if you are struggling for inspiration.

Four months to go
❏ **Buy your wedding lingerie:** Try it on under your dress to check that it doesn't show through. Also choose your going-away outfit and make sure that your dress fits perfectly.

❏ **Choose readers for the ceremony:** A good opportunity to involve guests who aren't in the wedding party.

❏ **Check menus:** Discuss the finer details of your menu with the caterers and check that the cake is going to be ready on time.

❏ **Inoculations:** Visit your doctor to find out if you need any inoculations for your honeymoon. Book future appointments.

❏ **Make/print directions and maps to the ceremony and reception:** Put them inside invitations so that your guests can't get lost.

Two months to go
❏ **Send out your invitations:** Remember to include an RSVP address and the map and directions of the venue if it's hard to find.

❏ **Buy a guest book:** This makes a wonderful record of the day.

❏ **Arrange rehearsal dinner:** Choose somewhere close to the venue, preferably a restaurant or hotel, which guests can easily get to and park at.

❏ **Have your programmes printed:** Check a sample copy first for spelling errors and colour corrections.

❏ **Hire a make-up artist and hairdresser for the wedding day:** Start discussing and practising different looks now.

❑ **Determine the reception layout:** This is the time for important decisions such as whether you're going to have a long top table or if you're going to have a dance floor.

❑ **Inform places like banks and building societies if you are changing your name:** You may need to send them proof of your name change, so you'll need extra copies of your marriage certificate.

❑ **Buy the certificate or licence from the registrar.**

Two weeks to go

❑ **Have your final dress fitting:** Take along your lingerie and shoes to be sure you're happy with the fit and overall look.

❑ **Confirm your seating plan and place cards:** Contact anyone who still hasn't RSVP'd to check whether or not they are coming.

❑ **Tell your caterer the final guest count:** They will need to be clear on numbers so that they can order in the right amount of food and drink – ask them to cater for a few extras just in case.

❑ **Give everyone involved a list of their duties on the wedding day:** This way they'll know exactly what they are supposed to be doing when, and won't have to keep asking you!

❑ **Buy gifts for the bridal party:** The gifts don't have to be elaborate, just heart-felt.

❑ **Break in your wedding shoes at home:** Wear them round the house as often as possible so you don't get blisters on the big day!

❑ **Check that the groom, best man and your father have all written speeches and are practising them:** Offer to be an audience for them, or, if you don't want hear them before the big day, ask your chief bridesmaid to check on their progress.

❑ **Check with your gift-list company that gifts have been marked off:** It's a good idea to keep your own records too about who has bought what as it makes the thank-you notes easier to write.

One week to go
❑ **Final meeting with florist and cake designer:** Check that everything is going according to plan.
❑ **Call your photographer/videographer/band to reconfirm time and date:** Speak to them in person rather than leaving a message.
❑ **Pick up your dress or have it delivered:** Hang it up immediately so that it won't crease, and put it safely in a clothes bag.
❑ **Make sure your groom has confirmed honeymoon arrangements:** Check where your passports are and that they are up to date.
❑ **Have a facial or spa day if you've got time:** It will help you to relax and make your skin look great on the day.

One day to go
❑ **Finalise your seating plan:** If you're worried about any family clashes, check the final plan with your mum.
❑ **Have a manicure and pedicure:** Get those nails in order so that they'll look picture-perfect on the day.
❑ **Final ceremony rehearsal and dinner:** Your final chance to ask the minister or officiant any burning questions about the big day, and a good opportunity to find out exactly what you have to do on the day.
❑ **Check that the groom/best man has finalised transport to and from the ceremony:** It's a good idea to time the route, and then allow an extra five minutes in case of traffic problems.

❑ **Arrange for the cake to be taken to the reception venue:** Ask your cake maker if he or she can bring it, in case there are any problems during the journey that mean it has to be styled again at the venue.

❑ **Send gifts:** Send members of the bridal party a small gift and note thanking them for their help on your special day.

The wedding day

❑ **Hair and make-up artist appointment:** You should arrange for your hairdresser and make-up artist to come as early as possible, just in case there are any last-minute hitches.

❑ **Post a thank-you letter and small gift to your parents:** Thank them for helping and tell them how much you love them.

❑ **RELAX and have fun – it's your wedding day!**

Chapter 2
Budgeting

You've got a plan of your dream wedding, but you've also got to decide how you are going to pay for that dream to become a reality. If you budget properly, it should be possible to buy that designer dress and have money left over for the cake and flowers – just don't get carried away.

Figuring it out

There's no getting away from it – weddings are expensive! A ceremony and reception in the UK costs on average a whopping £13,500, but there are lots of couples who spend half that sum and still have a fantastic day, so don't feel that the only way to do it properly is by breaking the bank.

The first thing you and your groom have to do is to sit down and work out exactly how much you have to spend. Pick a quiet time when you are both free and won't be disturbed, so you'll be able to concentrate fully on your finances.

You will have to decide who is going to pay for what, and whether you can rely on help from relatives or if you are going to pay for the day yourselves. Do you have savings, and do you want to spend them on the wedding day?

By now you are likely to have plumped for a wedding date, so it's time to make sure that your finances are going to co-ordinate with that time scale. If you've got six months, is that going to be enough time to save up what you need, or will you have to take out a loan? Remember, most companies will need deposits, so you're going to need some money to pay up front.

The most important thing is not to get into serious debt because of your wedding day. Not only will it put a damper on the big day, it will also be a harsh start to your new married life together. Keep everything in perspective: the emphasis of the day is on marrying your partner, not having the best party of the year, so technically it shouldn't matter where you wed or how much you spend on the reception.

Who pays for what?

Traditionally, the bride's parents paid for their clothes, the bridesmaids' and pageboys' outfits and the bride's dress. They paid for transport to the ceremony for the bride and her father and other members of their wedding party, and for transport to the reception for themselves and the groom's parents. They also helped out with the ceremony and reception venues, the rehearsal, the licence, food, drinks and entertainment.

The groom's family used to be expected to pay for the transport to the ceremony for the groom and best man and transport to the reception for the bride and groom. They also paid for the bride's bouquet and headdress, bridesmaids' flowers, buttonholes and corsages and any decorations for the cars during the day.

You, the lucky bride, were expected to fork out very little, but the groom's financial obligations included ceremony expenses such as the banns or marriage certificate, choir, bell-ringers, collection, minister or registrar. He also paid for the honeymoon, gifts for the best man and ushers, and the stag night.

If this traditional breakdown of who pays for what is not going to work in your circumstances, you're not alone! In reality, most modern couples are much more likely to want to pay for large sections of the wedding themselves. The jump in the average age of those getting married, from early 20s to early 30s, means that many more couples are now in a better financial position to pay for their wedding themselves when they finally decide to tie the knot, with maybe a little help from Mum and Dad. You may also prefer to fund your own wedding because it avoids the problem of parents wielding too much control over the type of ceremony and reception you can have because they are paying for it.

If either of your sets of parents is generously offering to pay for a large percentage of the wedding, be sure to draw up the ground rules early on. Money donations shouldn't mean that they automatically have the right to decide how the wedding will be, so make sure they understand from the outset that this is your day, not theirs.

How do we allocate our wedding budget?

You need to write a breakdown of your wedding day and allocate a percentage of your budget to each section. In most circumstances, the largest sum of money, around 50 per cent of your budget, is saved for the reception. This includes beverages, food, the cake, venue fee and entertainment. As a rough guide you should then allocate around 10 per cent of your budget to each of the remaining expenses: clothing, flowers, photography, music and stationery. These are estimates, and you will need to keep some cash spare for extras like gifts and transport, but it is a good starting point and covers all of the essentials.

Top tips on how to save money

Not everyone has £15,000 to spend on their wedding day, and some people simply may not want to. These days there are lots of ways to cut down the costs and still make it a magical day. Read below for helpful tips and keep a look out for advice on how to save money throughout the book.

The crucial thing is that this is your day. Spend your money in the way that you want to so you get the best possible day without a crippling bill at the end of it. You are a modern and independent bride – don't feel pressured by the multi-million-pound wedding industry!

1   For rule one, just remember: KISS. Keep It Simple, Stupid! Simple and stylish is by far the most effective solution.
2   Your dress doesn't have to cost the earth – these days there are some wonderful choices around that are the same price as a ballgown. High-street designs have come on leaps and bounds; some of the best shops include Monsoon, which sells beaded wedding gowns from under £200, and Debenhams, which has a dedicated wedding area full of beautiful dresses at affordable prices. Does your grandmother, mum or auntie have a vintage dress that they want to pass down? It will have tremendous sentimental value, and you could easily have it altered for a snip.
3   What about making your own dress, asking a friend to help or hiring a dressmaker? It allows you to design your dream dress and costs considerably less than many of the designer wedding boutiques – the only thing that you will need plenty of is time. Also keep an eye out for sales: many of the wedding shops sell off designer gowns for a fraction of their initial price when they are getting in new stock.

4   If you are having a traditional church wedding, you can share the costs of flowers with a couple getting married on the same day. Or ask the vicar for permission to decorate the church the day before your ceremony and get some friends to help.

5   Choose flowers that are in season, which are always cheaper, and avoid popular wedding flowers such as roses, which are expensive.

6   Do you really need a videographer? Perhaps you have a friend with a camcorder who would be willing to video the day for you.

7   Serve sparkling wine instead of champagne for the toasts and sparkling wine with orange juice when the guests arrive.

8   Serve a buffet instead of a sit-down three-course meal. You could ask close friends or relatives to help make some of the food.

9   If the venue has a bar, you should not be expected to pay for drinks all evening. Provide the first two drinks for free – or offer free drinks on arrival – and then ask guests to pay for any further rounds.

10 Serve your wedding cake as pudding – especially if you opt for something like chocolate cake rather than traditional fruitcake.

11 Cut costs on stationery by letting guests sit where they like on each table rather than paying for name tags at each place, or make your own on your PC. You could make your own order-of-service sheets and invitations, too.

12 Think about whether you really need to give out gifts to your guests. If you do, make your own favours: for example put a couple of Thorntons chocolates in a little box and tie it with ribbon.

13 For entertainment, why not ask friends to help out? Maybe one of them is into DJing or plays in a band. You could make up suitable compilation tapes or CDs yourself so you can just set them up and leave them to play. Or you could rent a karaoke machine!

Insurance

Buying wedding insurance is viewed by some as pessimistic and another bill on top of the already mounting expenses of the big day. However, it really is worth looking into if you are spending a lot of your money on the wedding party. Despite all your efforts, the unexpected may occur, such as a freak flood, over which you have no control, and you'll thank your lucky stars that you took out wedding insurance if the wedding has to be postponed or relocated.

When studying insurance policies, check that the basics are covered, such as ruined photographs, theft of presents, damage to your wedding dress and help if suppliers go bust and you lose your deposit. Draw up proper contracts with all of your suppliers as you'll only get money back if you can prove you have suffered loss against a contract. Insurance companies will need to see written evidence and that some kind of deposit has been made to ensure delivery of goods. All contracts, whether for your dress or your photographs, should include your basic wedding details: names, addresses, phone numbers, wedding date, venues, services to be provided, times, exact costs including VAT and any agreed extras.

☺ Get several quotes to compare prices, and check the small print.

Do we need a pre-nuptial agreement?

A pre-nuptial agreement is a legal contract listing exactly what you would both walk away with from the marriage in case of divorce. It's more common in the United States than in the UK, but it is on the increase on both sides of the Atlantic.

Pre-nuptial agreements are usually drawn up if one side, or both sides, of the couple has a significant amount of money, property or business to lose in the event of separation – both parties must agree to the terms. To some, it's seen as mercenary and a highly unromantic way to enter into marriage; to others, it's sensible and a necessity to protect their assets should anything go wrong with the marriage further down the line. If you are interested in a pre-nup, consult a lawyer, who will be able to advise you and draw up a water-tight contract. Approach the topic with tact and caution with your partner, however, as they're likely to see your move as casting doubt over your long-term prospects.

Budget checklist

You've decided how much you have to spend, and where you are allocating your budget, and it's important that you stick to that figure. Use this checklist to help you keep track of exactly what is being spent.

Clothing	Estimated	Actual
Bride's outfit		
Wedding gown		
Veil		
Shoes and hosiery		
Accessories		
Lingerie		
Going-away outfit		
Groom's outfit		
Suit		
Shirt		
Hat		
Shoes		

	Estimated	Actual
Accessories		
Going-away outfit		
Attendants' outfits (if paid for)		
Sub total		

Stationery
Invitations
Order-of-service sheets
Menus and place cards
Seating plan
Thank-you notes
Sub total

Flowers
Bride's bouquet
Bridesmaids' posies
Buttonholes/corsages
Ceremony flowers
Reception flowers
Sub total

Ceremony
Music
Church/venue fees
Photographer
Videographer
Licence
Sub total

Reception	Estimated	Actual
Music/entertainment		
Venue hire		
Drink		
Food		
Cake		
Favours/confetti		
Sub total		
Other		
Insurance		
Gifts for wedding party		
First-night hotel		
Honeymoon		
Sub total		
Total Costs		
Clothing		
Stationery		
Flowers		
Ceremony		
Reception		
Other		
TOTAL		

Chapter 3
The Ceremony

Before you decide any other wedding details, you need to start at the very beginning and decide what sort of ceremony you're going to have. Not only is it going to set the tone of the whole day, it must also relate to the beliefs you both hold. There is so much choice these days that you don't need to rule anything out when it comes to tying the knot. If you're both footie mad, why not get hitched at your local stadium? Or you could escape to the wilds and marry in a castle.

There is no correct set formula to wedding ceremonies, because every one is unique and you'll want to give it your personal touch, but we can tell you the basic options that are available and how to go about booking your venue.

What are our ceremony choices?
For your marriage to be recognised, the wedding must be solemnised by an authorised person: a superintendent registrar, an ordained minister of the Church of England or an ordained minister of another religion.

Your basic options are a church ceremony, a civil wedding in a licensed building, a civil wedding in a register office or a ceremony abroad. You could have a humanist ceremony, but it isn't legally recognised, so you would need to marry in a register office first before holding your own ceremony. The marriage should take place, by law, between 8am and 6pm, except for Jewish and Quaker ceremonies, which are performed under special licence.

We're from different faiths, what should we do?

If you're religious then you're going to want a ceremony that reflects your faith, and inevitably this means that you will want to exchange vows in a place of worship relevant to your religion. If you are from different religious backgrounds, this needn't mean that one of you has to back down. There are a number of options.

You could be married in one religion and then receive a blessing in the other, or ask your vicar, priest or rabbi about an inter-faith marriage, which would keep you and, no doubt, your parents happy. If one of you is Catholic and the other isn't, it is usually acceptable for you to marry in a Catholic Church whilst agreeing to certain conditions, unless you are divorced. If you are Jewish, an orthodox rabbi will not marry you unless your partner converts to Judaism.

A church ceremony

Obviously, Christian couples will want a church ceremony. Some other couples also want a church ceremony even if they aren't regular churchgoers because they feel it is the most appropriate place to exchange vows due to the solemnity and reverence.

How do we arrange a church ceremony?

Technically, you can be married in a church as long as you are both single and at least one of you lives in, or is on the electoral register of, the parish of your chosen church.

However, you can't simply book a church. You must approach the minister with your request, and have a chat about your plans and desire to have a church ceremony. He or she may not mind that you aren't in the congregation every week, but be prepared to be asked to attend services in the run-up to your wedding. The fact that you may not attend church regularly doesn't necessarily mean that you won't be allowed to marry there; but you should respect the fact that the minister will want to discuss your religious convictions with you.

If you're divorced, it is highly unlikely that a minister or priest will allow you to marry in the Church of England or Catholic Church, although each case is individual and it is worth talking to your vicar to see if they would make an exception. Methodists and Baptists tend to take a less strict stance.

How soon in advance should we arrange the ceremony?

If the minister agrees and you are given the go-ahead to marry in church, he or she will then read out the banns – publication of your intention to marry – for three consecutive Sundays. Once this has been done, you must tie the knot within three months of the banns being read out. If you don't, you will have to go through the procedure again. Banns are the sole legal necessity for a church wedding.

The minister who performs the ceremony acts as registrar on behalf of the state and as priest on behalf of the Church. After the banns have been read out, you'll be given a certificate, which allows you to marry.

You'll need to discuss with the minister the type of ceremony you want. You will need to decide which hymns you would like, whether you will be hiring a choir and what readings to have. It is advisable to have a rehearsal of the ceremony before the big day, so that everyone knows exactly where they should be standing and what they should be saying. It is common these days for the minister to want to spend time with a couple to discuss the implications of marriage, particularly if they are not regular churchgoers.

What's the running order of a church ceremony?
The arrival
The guests will arrive first, the groom's family and friends sitting on the right and your party on the left. It's then usual for the groom to arrive with the best man, just before the allocated time, and wait at the end of the aisle by the altar. You arrive last of all, traditionally accompanied by your father. If this isn't possible, or you simply don't want to be 'given away', there's nothing to stop you walking down the aisle by yourself, or asking your mum or best friend to accompany you.

Introduction and welcome
The minister will welcome everyone to the ceremony, pray for the couple and then declare the purposes of marriage before asking if anyone knows of any reason why the marriage cannot take place, which has to be done by law.

The declaration
You'll be asked to declare, before God, your families and friends that you will love, comfort, honour and protect each other and be faithful as long as you both shall live. Brides used to agree to obey their husbands but the modern service does not include this; the choice of which wording to use is yours.

You'll then turn to each other and repeat the vows below. As you take it in turns to speak, you'll hold your partner's right hand, symbolising the joining of your two lives.

'To have and to hold, from this day forward, for better, for worse, for richer, for poorer, in sickness and in health, to love and to cherish, till death do us part.'

The ring exchange
Rings are a symbol of unending love, and by exchanging them you are completing your promises to one another. At the end of the ceremony you will both say:
'With this ring I thee wed, with my body I thee worship, and with all my worldly goods I thee endow...'

Proclamation
The minister or priest pronounces you husband and wife and says that the groom may kiss the bride. You'll then usually go to a separate room to sign the register in front of two witnesses and then return to the church, where you may want to have a hymn or other music played before departing from the church.

At-a-glance running order
- Processional
- Opening statements
- Wedding reading or prayer
- Charge to the couple
- Questions of willingness
- Presentation of the bride
- Exchange of vows
- Blessing and presentation of the rings
- Declaration of marriage
- Signing of the register
- Wedding prayer
- The Lord's Prayer
- Recessional

A civil ceremony

You can have a civil wedding at any venue that has been licensed. There are currently around 3000 premises, which vary widely, from hotels to castles, and football clubs to racecourses.

A civil ceremony is ideal if you don't want a religious ceremony, if you want more flexibility for the service or if you want to hold your ceremony and reception in the same venue. Pretty much anything goes in terms of what you can do and say at a civil ceremony, so if you really want to walk up the aisle to the theme from *Star Wars,* you can. However, the ceremony cannot include any hymns or readings with a religious content.

☺ In Scotland, a Christian ceremony can take place almost anywhere, as it is the minister conducting the ceremony who is licensed. A Scottish civil ceremony can only take place in a register office.

British law currently says that a venue has to be licensed in order for a couple to tie the knot there. However, in the next couple of years there will be moves to make the person marrying couples licensed rather than the venue, which will give people a much greater choice as to where they can get married. So, if you have always fancied saying 'I do' on the top of a mountain or on the top deck of the number 42, it may be worth holding out for a couple of years.

You also have a lot more options in terms of what you can say and do in a civil ceremony, such as writing your own vows, playing any kind of music and generally giving it the personal touch.

Who do I contact to arrange a civil ceremony?

If you choose to have a civil ceremony you should contact the superintendent registrar of the district where you want to marry (see page 178 for telephone numbers of General Register Offices). If you want to get wed in a licensed venue, you should also contact them. The fees for the attendance of the superintendent registrar and a registrar for a marriage at an approved premises are set by the local authority, so you'll need to contact them individually to find out prices. On the day of the wedding, you'll need at least two people to act as witnesses.

What's the running order of a civil ceremony?
Arrival
The guests arrive at the venue and are ushered into the room where the ceremony will take place. It's usual for people to sit where they like, although places are often reserved for close family at the front. As with a church ceremony, it's usual for the groom to arrive there early and the bride to arrive last, to music of your choice.

Welcome and introduction
The celebrant welcomes guests to the ceremony and explains what will happen during the proceedings. The speech is likely to include a reminder of the importance of the vows that are about to be exchanged and also the words: 'if any person here present knows of a lawful impediment why they should not be joined in matrimony, declare it now'. You can discuss with your celebrant beforehand what they will say in the speech, and anything that you would like included.

The bride and groom declare their intention to marry
You can write your own words for this, or ask your officiant for advice or a sample ceremony which will read something like 'Will you take (groom's/bride's name) to be your lawful wedded wife/husband, to be faithful, loving and loyal to him/her for the rest of your lives together?' This would be answered with 'I will'.

The marriage vows
To make the marriage official, you've got to say a legally required vow, such as: 'I do solemnly declare that I know not of any lawful impediment why I (bride's/groom's name) may not be joined in matrimony to (bride's/groom's name).'

Ring exchange
The symbolic exchange of the rings at the end of the ceremony is usually just as much a part of a civil ceremony as it is of a religious one. It can be accompanied by a declaration of love for one another, and promises to care for each other for better or for worse.

The signing of the register
The register is usually signed in front of the guests and overseen by the marriage registrar, who may say a speech at the beginning of the proceedings, which could include: '(groom's name), you may now kiss the bride.'

At-a-glance running order
- Arrival of the bride
- Welcome and introduction
- Bride and groom declare intention to marry
- Vows of marriage
- Exchange of rings
- Signing of the register

What's the quickest way to get married?
The quickest and most economical way to get married in the 21st century is at a register office. It is an ideal choice if you are not interested in a huge ceremony and want to get married as soon as possible.

You can marry at any register office, so you are not restricted to the one closest to where you live. When you have decided where you're going to tie the knot, you must inform the superintendent registrar up to three months before the date on which you want to marry. He will inform you that you can choose to marry by certificate or by licence. Licence is quicker, but more expensive. It is required that one of you has lived in the registration district for at least 15 days prior to giving notice, but then the marriage can take place after only one day of giving notice. Make sure that you have documents to show the superintendent registrar. These may include your passports and other identification. If you're divorced, you'll need to show a decree absolute.

Certificate is the most common form of notice and requires that you've lived in the registration district for at least seven days prior to giving notice to the register office. It's then a further 21 days before the marriage can take place. If you or your partner live in different districts, you'll need to give notice in both. Both certificate and licence are valid for up to three months.

Register offices vary from town to town, but they are usually simply furnished with chairs for family and a small number of friends to sit and watch the proceedings. If you want to personalise your ceremony, most register offices will allow you to play your choice of pre-recorded music, or to bring in a few flowers to decorate the room. Bear in mind, though, that the ceremony will only last about 10 minutes and that you will have to clear the room for the next couple.

Ceremony abroad

If the idea of saying your vows next to a turquoise sea beneath blue skies and in guaranteed sunshine is more appealing to you than getting hitched in a draughty church, then you could join the 30,000 other UK couples who are jetting off to marry overseas each year.

This option is becoming increasingly popular for a number of reasons besides the sunshine. These include the sense of adventure and the chance to have a week-long celebration and a hassle-free wedding day which avoids family politics. For many couples it also makes economic sense. With an average foreign wedding costing less than £5000 – including the honeymoon – it falls way below the average price for a UK wedding.

A wedding abroad is simple to organise, provided you do all of your homework and preparations well in advance in the UK. The simplest option of all is to hand over the stress to a tour operator, preferably one that specialises in weddings overseas. Most of the big groups, like First Choice, Cosmos and Kuoni, have dedicated wedding co-ordinators on their staff, who will discuss where you want to go and will arrange your wedding in detail.

Where should we go?

Popular destinations for weddings include Sri Lanka, the Caribbean, the Seychelles, Mauritius, the Maldives, South Africa (particularly safari lodges) and Cyprus. North America is also a favourite, especially for couples who want to get hitched in a more unconventional way, like underwater in Florida, or in a hot-air balloon above Las Vegas! If you need inspiration, good sources of information include travel agents, bridal magazines and the internet.

If you are worried about arrangements once you get there, it's a good idea to pick a hotel or resort where there is a dedicated wedding co-ordinator who will oversee everything. They will be able to take care of your cake, flowers and drinks, and will also be able to advise you on paperwork and licences.

> ☺ Many resorts have a free wedding package, but do check exactly what you are getting and what costs extra. For example, photography or live music can often be an expensive addition to your ceremony.

Who can arrange it?

Most good tour operators should be able to advise you on any legal requirements for getting married at your chosen destination. You may be required to bring certain documentation, such as a decree absolute if one of you is divorced, or a birth certificate, or to take a blood test. It is also a common requirement to have been resident in the country in which you want to marry for four days or more before you can tie the knot. It's therefore common for couples to have a week's holiday before marrying and then honeymooning.

Readings

Readings should reflect your feelings for one another and be appropriate for the type of wedding you are planning. They're also a great way to involve close family and friends in your important day. Remember that the person you choose will be in the spotlight, so think carefully about your choice and ask someone who doesn't mind taking centre stage and who is, preferably, used to public speaking.

What readings are appropriate for a church ceremony?

There are lots of readings to choose from, but bear in mind that a church ceremony is more solemn and formal than a civil ceremony so you will need to choose something in keeping with the surroundings. Consult with your vicar or priest to see what is acceptable and to ask them if they have any recommendations.

> ☺ You may want to choose readings from scriptures, such as 1 Corinthians 13:1–13, Psalm 23 or John 15.9–17. Other popular readings include 'Epithalamion' by Edmund Spenser and Song of Solomon 4:10–11.

What are good readings for a civil ceremony?

These readings don't usually have any religious connotations, but you can check with your registrar before the wedding that what you have chosen is appropriate. You may be surprised at what is considered appropriate, as it can vary according to registrars and how flexible they are. Popular choices include the 'Eskimo Love Song', 'A Dedication To My Wife' by TS Eliot, 'Sonnet 116' by William Shakespeare and 'A Red, Red Rose' by Robert Burns.

> ☺ If you can't find a reading to reflect your feelings adequately, you could always have a go at penning your own. Or what about commissioning a professional poet to write an original ode to your partner? It is an incredibly romantic gift for your wedding day.

Ceremony music

Choosing music for your ceremony is an important task. It is the soundtrack for one of the most important days of your life, so you are going to want to get it spot on, and also ensure that it is a true reflection of yourselves.

The easiest way to deal with the issue of ceremony music is to break it down into individual moments, rather than trying to think of an hour's worth of music. For example, what sort of music do you want to arrive to? What sounds do you want to walk back down the aisle to?

It is also important to select the right music for the venue you have chosen – for example, is it a very modern building, or an ancient church? When you have a sense of the mood of your surroundings and of what you want to create, it makes the task much easier.

Don't feel that you can't mix different styles of music, however. There is nothing to stop you beginning with some classical pieces by a composer such as Bach, then choosing a more contemporary tune for when you walk back down the aisle. Another option is a favourite piece of music, or a song that means something to both of you.

Once you have decided on the styles of music that you want during the ceremony, you will have a better idea as to whether you need musicians or a choir. Popular choices for weddings include string quartets, jazz bands, classical guitars and solo singers.

☺ If you want pre-recorded music, make sure that your venue has an adequate sound system.

Music suggestions

	Traditional	Contemporary
Prelude	'Water Music', Handel 'Air on the G String', Bach 'Jesu Joy of Man's Desiring', Bach 'Largo', Handel 'The Arrival of the Queen of Sheba', Handel	'Unchained Melody', Righteous Brothers 'When I Fall in Love', Nat King Cole 'Fields of Gold', Sting
Processional	Fanfare, Purcell 'Wedding March', Mozart 'Wedding Chorus', Wagner 'Trumpet Voluntary', Clarke	'The Look of Love', Andy Williams 'Have I Told You Lately', Van Morrison 'Can't Take My Eyes off of You', Frankie Valli
Interlude	'Arioso', Bach 'Ave Maria', Schubert 'The Call', Vaughan Williams	'Wonderful World', Louis Armstrong 'Unconditional', Will Ackerman 'All I Ask of You', from *Phantom of the Opera* 'Takes My Breath Away', Tuck and Patti

Recessional	'Wedding March', Mendelssohn	'All You Need is Love', The Beatles
	'Water Music', Handel	'Stand By Me', Ben E King
	'Trumpet tune in C', Purcell	'It Had To Be You', Frank Sinatra
	'Ode to Joy', Beethoven	

What happens at the end of the ceremony?

It's all too easy to concentrate on the ceremony itself and forget about what happens after you've walked back down the aisle. If you're having a church wedding you could arrange for a peal of bells to ring out as you exit the church; it's a magical sound and is a fantastic way of announcing that you've tied the knot.

You could leave your guests to mingle outside the venue before moving on to the reception, but rather than just having them standing around, you could get them to join in the celebration by throwing confetti. The ushers can hand the confetti around to guests, or guest can help themselves from a basket as they leave the venue.

☺ Paper confetti is not allowed at most venues because it's difficult to clean up and can stain fabric when wet. Good alternatives are rose petals, biodegradable rice paper or even bubbles. If you opt for the traditional rice – a symbol of fertility – remember it should be thrown up into the air to fall *gently* on to the couple!

Chapter 4
Stationery

The amount of stationery you are going to need will depend on the size of your wedding. For a small, intimate event, this is not going to be a huge drain on your budget, whereas for a large, formal wedding, it will need a bigger spend. The key basics that you'll need to cover are invitations, reply cards, orders of service, menus, seating plans and place cards.

Invitations

Invites are the first thing your guests are going to see from your special day, so you'll want to be sure that they are a reflection of the style of wedding that you're planning.

Where can I buy wedding invitations?

Traditional designs are usually black type on cream or white card, but popular, modern choices like flowers, photographs of the couple and even cartoons are both fun and eye-catching.

If you've got a certain idea of how they should look, you may want to commission a designer to make your invites. There are lots of companies all over the country who will handcraft your designs, but be warned, prices will probably be £3 plus per invite.

Don't forget to check out the high-street options too, particularly if you're on a tight budget.

What about the writing?

For small, intimate weddings, you could hand write the cards yourself, or if you've got a computer at home with a good choice of fonts, you could use that. If your handwriting really isn't up to it, however, you could consider hiring a calligrapher, who will add a very stylish edge to your stationery. Ask for samples of their work and give them enough time to complete the job.

For larger weddings where a lot of stationery is needed, it is advisable to get the invitations printed. There are several options available, the most expensive being hand-engraved. Thermographed, which is made to look like it has been hand-engraved, is a cheaper method, while flat-printed is the least expensive choice.

> ☺ Check all of the wording very carefully before you agree to a large number being printed. Once it's been done, you won't be able to make changes without huge extra costs.

When do we send the invitations?

Invitations are usually sent out around three months before the wedding, so you need to be organised, and choose and order them around five to six months in advance if they are being commissioned.

> ☺ It's usual to send an invitation to the groom's mother and father, and to the minister if you're having a church wedding.

Can we ask people not to bring children on the invites?

If children are invited, they should be named on the invitation. Be tactful, be consistent and be clear about what you want.

Is it a good idea to send save-the-date cards?

Sending out cards to ask guests to book your wedding date in their diaries well in advance of the big day is a great idea, as it means they will know not to book any holidays or say 'yes' to other wedding invitations on that date. They don't have to be fancy, just a card with your names, the announcement and the date of the wedding. Just remember to put a note on it that the official invitation will follow, which will have an RSVP on it.

Wording for invitations

If you're sending an invitation to a married couple, it is traditional to use the husband's name, such as 'Mr and Mrs David Brown', while if it is to a family, it should include the children's first names, for example 'Mr and Mrs David Brown, Edward and Tom'.

Below are some standard wordings for wedding invites to act as a guide, but as with everything involved in your wedding, if you want to make it more personal or unusual, go ahead!

Traditional

Mr and Mrs Robert Smith request the pleasure of ...
at the marriage of their daughter Emma
to
Mr Nick Collins
at St Paul's Church, Hereford
on Saturday, 26th August, 2003
at 2pm
and afterwards at
The Old Swan Hotel, Hereford

Bridal couple as host
Miss Emma Smith and Mr Nick Collins request the pleasure of…
at their marriage at St Paul's Church, Hereford
on Saturday, 26th August, 2003
at 2pm
and afterwards at
The Old Swan Hotel

Remarried mother as host
Mr and Mrs John Brown
request the pleasure of…
at the marriage of her daughter Emma
to
Mr Nick Collins
at St Paul's Church, Hereford
on Saturday, 26th August, 2003
at 2pm
and afterwards at The Old Swan Hotel, Hereford

Remarried father as host
Mr and Mrs Robert Smith
request the pleasure of…
at the marriage of his daughter Emma
to
Mr Nick Collins
at St Paul's Church, Hereford
on Saturday, 26th August, 2003
at 2pm
and afterwards at
The Old Swan Hotel, Hereford

Widowed parent as host

Mrs Robert Smith
requests the pleasure of…
at the marriage of her daughter Emma
to
Mr Nick Collins
at St Paul's Church, Hereford
on Saturday, 26th August, 2003
at 2pm
and afterwards at
The Old Swan Hotel, Hereford

Divorced parents as host

Mr Robert Smith and Mrs Sue Cook
request the pleasure of…
at the marriage of their daughter Emma
to
Mr Nick Collins
at St Paul's Church, Hereford
on Saturday, 26th August, 2003
at 2pm
and afterwards at
The Old Swan Hotel, Hereford

Without name host

The pleasure of…
is requested at the marriage of Miss Emma Smith
and
Mr Nick Collins
at St Paul's Church, Hereford
on Saturday, 26th August, 2003
at 2pm
and afterwards at
The Old Swan Hotel, Hereford

Reception-only invitation

Mr and Mrs Robert Smith request the pleasure of…
at a reception at The Old Swan Hotel, Hereford
on Saturday, 26th August, 2003
at 5pm
following the marriage of their daughter Emma to
Mr Nick Collins

Maps and reply cards

When you send out the invitations, it's a good idea to include a map of how to find the venue, and also any information about nearby hotels if you've got guests coming from out of town.

Reply cards are useful to include with the invitations because they do encourage guests to answer more promptly. However, there's nothing wrong with including RSVP and the address to which the guest has to reply at the bottom left-hand corner of the invitations.

Orders of service

These are more common if you are having a church wedding, as they allow guests to know exactly what is going on throughout the ceremony and usually include information about any music, readings and hymns that will take place during the ceremony. It is also a good idea to include the words of any hymns or songs on the service sheet so your guests can follow along without having to fumble through a book.

You'll need one sheet for every one of your guests, and you should commission your order-of-service sheets at least six weeks before the wedding day so that there is plenty of time to make any corrections or changes, and also for them to be printed in bulk.

> ☺ Don't forget that if you have a PC and an eye for style, you can easily create your own orders of service.

The order-of-service cards should reflect the tone of your day: formal black text on white card if it's a traditional wedding, more colour and drawings if you've opted for a contemporary wedding. It's usual to have the name of the bride and groom on the front, along with the name of the church and the date and time of the ceremony. If you want to be more adventurous, you could match the sheet to the colours and style of the rest of your wedding stationery, or you could commission an illustration for the cover, such as one of the venue where you're tying the knot.

Some couples now include an order-of-the-day sheet inside the order-of-service sheet, listing times of what will be happening throughout the day, such as the speeches and cutting of the cake. This is a great way to ensure your guests know exactly what is going on and also a lovely memento to remind them of your wedding day.

☺ It's a good idea to have 15 extra copies of your order-of-service sheets printed for any unexpected visitors who may attend and to ensure you have one as a keepsake.

Menus

Menus are optional. If you're having a small buffet or serving up canapés then there is no need to go to the expense, although it might be advisable to have a large menu at the start of a buffet, listing what is on offer in case of any special dietary requirements your guests may have. If you are having a seated meal, you can opt to have individual menus at each place setting or one large menu for the whole table. Individual menus can be taken home and are a great reminder of the day, but they are far from essential and do add to the cost – some people would prefer another glass of wine!

Seating plans

If you're having a sit-down meal, you're going to need a plan showing guests where they are sitting – otherwise the wedding breakfast could descend into chaos as guests jostle for positions! The best option is to display your seating plan on a large board near the reception. Alternatively, you could write guests' names and table numbers on cards and lay them out on a tray where people can pick them up as they wander into the reception. If you do decide to go with this option, make sure that your tables are clearly numbered.

☺ Don't put your seating plan right by the entrance to the reception, as you tend to get a bottleneck where people gather round to try and see their position which prevents other guests from getting to their seats.

Place cards

If you do opt for a seating plan, you're also going to need place cards at the table, so guests know exactly where they are sitting as well as the table they are on. If you want to save money, but not time, you can easily make these yourselves with some folded cream or white card and good handwriting, or print them from your PC. If you want the wedding to co-ordinate perfectly, you can arrange to have your place cards made to match the menu, table plan and invitations – many printers will lower their prices if you are ordering items in bulk.

Some brides combine place cards and favours – tiny gifts for the wedding guests – a very sensible and stylish idea. Chic ideas include a little box of chocolates with a name tag attached, a heart-shaped cookie with the guest's name iced on to it, or how about a miniature bottle of whisky or brandy with the guest's name on the label?

Extras

If you really want to go to town, you could also order hymn book markers, gift tags and personalised letterheads with both of your names and address at the top. Some people also have thank-you cards printed to send out to guests instead of a handwritten letter, but you should think about whether filling in their name on a dotted line sends the same grateful message to the recipient as a thoughtful, personal note.

Chapter 5
Style and Beauty

Whether you are a less-is-more kind of girl or a dress-up-to-the-nines babe, you're going to want to look a million dollars on the big day. Your style will very much depend on your personality and the type of wedding you have.

Don't let anyone talk you into a look that you aren't happy with just because it's what you think a bride should be like on her wedding day. If your mum has always wanted her little girl to walk up the aisle looking like Lady Di but your idea of a wedding outfit is a body-skimming Dolce & Gabbana corset and skirt, don't be afraid to speak out – you're only doing this once, so it should be on your terms.

Equally, don't think you have to go for a cutting-edge look to keep up your image if in your heart of hearts you'd love to float down the aisle in a cloud of silk and organza.

When it comes to style and beauty, it's always a good idea to have your best friends around, as you're going to need some sound advice from people you trust. Ultimately though, this is about your big day so go for what you look and feel comfortable in.

The dress

Bias-cut, ballgown, A-line or empire-line, there's a dress out there to suit everyone. In fact, there's so much choice, it can be hard to know where to begin to find the outfit of your dreams. You always hear stories about girls who put on the first dress they see and it looks fantastic and fits like a glove, but the reality for most women is that it's going to take a few weeks or months of trawling around the shops to track down the dress that's going to take his breath away.

Don't be afraid to let your personality and style shine through. If a traditional wedding gown isn't for you, there are lots of alternatives. A trouser suit is an incredibly chic option, and a long satin coat is particularly lovely in winter. A short shift dress or a coloured gown could be just the way to stamp your individual taste on the day.

Where can I get inspiration for my dream dress?

Your inspiration for your dress, as with the rest of the wedding, can come from lots of different influences. The best place to start is at home. You'll have an idea about what you look best in, and if you have a favourite dress, consider what it is about that outfit that makes you feel special. Is it the cut, the colour, or simply that you had a great time in it?

You may also want to focus on the time of year that you're getting married. Brides tend to gravitate towards cool silk and chiffon for summer, but heavier velvets and satins for winter. You may gain inspiration from your wedding venue. If you're tying the knot in a castle, for example, you could have a medieval-inspired gown.

A good place to start searching for images of your dream dress are fashion mags and wedding magazines, as they'll show all the latest designs and provide information on how to get hold of a particular dress that you like.

Your budget will also dictate to some extent the type of dress you choose.

Wedding gowns can start from as little as £200 or £300 on the high street and soar up to £15,000 plus for a top-of-the-range designer dress. If you have £500 plus to blow on the gown, it's worth grabbing your maid of honour and heading for some dedicated bridal stores where you'll be guaranteed a very personal service and a wide selection of international gowns. Most stores ask you to make an appointment so that an assistant can be on hand to help you to try on the gowns and to discuss your preferences and budget. It's a good idea to take along someone whose opinion you trust, as a second point of view is always helpful, and it also makes it a more fun day out.

If you don't have a huge budget, then consider visiting high-street stores, many of which have fabulous gowns on offer for a fraction of the price of a designer dress. Particularly good are Debenhams, which has a separate bridal department, and Monsoon, which always has a small but beautiful array of beaded dresses for under £200. It is worth keeping an eye out for bridal shop sales, as you can pick up gowns for a third of their original price when stores clear their stock.

For something a bit different, check out vintage clothing stores or look out for classified adverts in local papers, which often feature second-hand wedding dresses for sale. You could also have your gown made by a dressmaker, which is usually a cheaper alternative to buying a new designer outfit. If you have a very limited amount to spend on the dress, you could hire a fantastic outfit for the day: after all, you're not going to be wearing it again.

☺ Remember to check out how your dress looks from behind as well as face on. Your guests will be looking at your back for most of the ceremony, so it should be as sensational as the front.

Do I need a dress contract?

What is a dress contract? Basically, it's an agreement about the details of what you are buying. If you're buying off the peg, the answer is no. However, if you're spending a lot of money having a dress made for you, then it's advisable. Drawing up a contract with your details and the details of the dress will put your mind at rest and allow you some comeback if it doesn't come in the exact style, colouring or size that you had requested. You can minimise any potential problems, though, by making sure that you choose a reputable designer and order your dress at least six months in advance of the wedding day, so that they will have enough time to buy in materials, make the gown and carry out fittings and alterations.

> ☺ Don't diet excessively between choosing your dress and the big day or your dress will be far too big. Similarly, don't order a dress a size too small and aim to diet to get into it – if you don't manage it, you'll be bursting at the seams.

What style of wedding dress will best suit my body shape?

Let's be honest here. There are very few people who are as thin and tall as a super model; in fact, most of us have some part of our body we're not keen on, whether it's the size of our bum or our non-existent shoulders. Well, cast all this aside when choosing your wedding dress, and concentrate on your best features. Whether it's your graceful back or your swan-like neck, you're going to be hunting for a dress that enhances your best features and hides the ones you're not so keen on. Follow this basic guide to discover what suits your body type.

Large hips and bust/tall

A ballgown-style dress, with a large skirt, nipped-in waist and long bodice is ideal because it can balance your body out. If you are busty up top and want to appear smaller than you are or divert attention away from your chest, then wear a scoop neck as it miraculously reduces it in size. Avoid any ruffles or bows around the neckline, which draw immediate attention to your chest. Alternatively, if you want to show off your assets, you could opt for a bustier, which will certainly get you noticed. A full skirt helps to define the waist. If you're worried about a sticking out stomach, look for a flat-fronted bodice, which will make you look like you're a gym regular!

Pear shape/short

If you're the classic English pear shape – small up top with larger hips and bum – then your ideal dress shape is the Empire-line. It is flattering because it has a seam directly under the bust, so emphasising your chest, but then drops straight to the floor without following the curves of the body, so disguising the hips and waist. The length of flowing fabric will also give you a tall silhouette. If you have wide hips, it is best to avoid anything that fits too closely over them, and don't draw attention to them with bustles or make them appear wider by wearing a tiered skirt.

Straight up and down/tall

Bias-cut is the least forgiving of all the bridal-dress styles, and is the one for you if you're tall and slim and not afraid to show off any curves. This cut literally hugs the body from top to bottom, although it should never look too tight. If you want to make yourself look a little bigger than you are, opt for a heavier fabric. This is not the dress for anyone top- or bottom-heavy. If you're tall and slim and want to look like you have some curves, a strapless design will work wonders – the top emphasises the bust and elongates the neck, while a nipped-in waist and full skirt will give you a curvier silhouette.

Stocky/short
The Princess-line is a miracle dress shape as it suits pretty much everyone. It's particularly good for disguising the classic English pear shape, short waists and chunky legs, as it hugs at the top and flares out like an A-line at the bottom, but doesn't have a waist so seems to lengthen the body and make you appear taller.

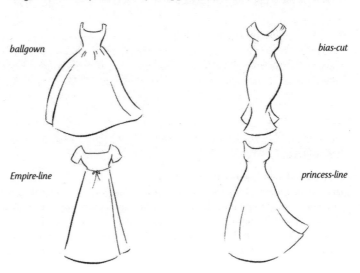

ballgown

bias-cut

Empire-line

princess-line

Should I have sleeves on my dress?

This will depend on how you feel about your arms. Some women hate exposing their upper arms, to others it's no problem, so opt for something that you feel comfortable with. If you're worried that your arms are chubby and you don't want to reveal them, choose a light, pretty fabric for the sleeve, such as chiffon or organza, which isn't skin-tight. If you have very short arms, three-quarter length sleeves will appear to lengthen them. If you're having a winter wedding and are worried about the cold, but still want a sleeveless or strapless gown, you could buy a sweeping coat to match your outfit that you can remove at the reception.

Should I have my dress made?

It may seem like an extravagance, but this can actually be a cheaper option. Some brides also have a gown made specifically for them because they can't find the dress of their dreams, or if they have found it, it's way out of their price range.

If you're employing a dressmaker – look for one in the Yellow Pages or on the internet – then you'll need to have an idea of the style of dress you want, and you'll also have to buy the fabric. It's useful for the dressmaker if you can take along a picture of the sort of gown you like.

As when buying a gown from a boutique, you can take into account the season that you're marrying in and your venue. It's important that you choose your style and fabric up to six months before the wedding to allow the dressmaker plenty of time to cut, alter and fit the dress and for you to be absolutely sure that it is the perfect one for you.

What is the best fabric for a wedding dress?

Silk is always a popular choice for bridal wear because it feels luxurious and is so light it won't feel hot no matter how long you wear it or how high the temperatures rise. On the downside, it is expensive and also creases very easily – who can forget Lady Diana's scrunched and dishevelled silk gown and train when she climbed out of the carriage to marry Prince Charles?

To avoid excessive creasing, many designers use Duchesse satin, which is a rich, heavy fabric that holds its shape much better than pure silk. Also popular are shantung and dupion. Increasingly popular are sheer fabrics like organza and tulle, which look fabulous when used as wraps or layering over silk gowns.

When picking the fabric of your dress, it is important to think about when you'll be wearing it. If your wedding is going to be in the height of summer, when temperatures are hopefully high, it's advisable to choose something that is lightweight that won't make you hot and bothered. Likewise, if you're saying 'I do' in the middle of winter, it makes sense to go for a thicker, richer fabric which is going to keep you warm. Many brides who are having a winter wedding opt for a wedding gown with a coat to keep them snug when they have to venture outside. Great fabrics for winter outfits include velvet and Duchesse satin. Don't be afraid to mix fabrics; a lace bodice with a satin skirt, or a cashmere top teamed with a beautiful silk skirt may not be conventional, but will look absolutely stunning.

☺ Choosing man-made fabrics is a good way of keeping the overall cost of your wedding dress down.

Should I get married in white?

We all know that traditional wedding dresses are white, but if white isn't right, then don't be afraid to experiment with colour. White is particularly unflattering if you have a very pale complexion as it will make you look washed out. If you want to look traditional, but also have colour in your cheeks, then consider a flattering ivory or cream.

Popular modern colours include gold, lilac and peach, which complement most skin types. Silver is flattering for olive, black and Asian skin, but will drain pale complexions of colour. Fair skin and hair looks great offset with pale blues and pinks. If you really want to stand out from the crowd, you could go for an eye-catching colour like red or burgundy, but if you're opting for a bright shade, it's advisable to keep detail and embellishments to a minimum.

It's all about you!

If you are despairing of finding a dress to suit you, just remember that you have a wardrobe full of clothes that look great on you. You may not feel like a fairy princess when you're trying on dresses in a cramped changing room, but just wait until your wedding day, when you'll be radiating so much happiness and confidence that the dress just becomes an accessory that you shine out of.

Dress care

Okay, so you're only wearing your wedding dress for a few hours, but if you want it to remain immaculate, take note of these indispensable tips on how to care for it.

- As soon as your dress enters your house, hang it up so that the creases will fall out.

- Use a padded, strong hanger to keep it in shape.
- Cover your dress up so that it won't get marked or dusty.
- Ask your chief bridesmaid to carry a stick of white chalk with her so that you can quickly lighten any marks that you get on the day.
- Brush away any confetti that lands on your gown as quickly as possible, as it can stain when wet.
- Sponge off any champagne or wine stains as quickly as possible as they can leave a brown mark.
- Have your dress professionally dry cleaned as soon as you can after the honeymoon so that stains don't become unmovable.
- Store the gown covered in tissue paper in a large box, not a pvc cover, and stuff the bodice with paper to avoid permanent creases. Store it away in a dark cupboard.
- Check it once a year for any damage or changes.

☺ Don't store your dress in an attic as you don't want mice to nest in it or nibble away at it.

Lingerie

Your dress is what's on show, but what you wear underneath it is just as important. Good underwear can transform the shape of a body and the shape of clothing, so it's worth investing in some good lingerie.

It's a good idea to buy the lingerie after you've chosen the style of your dress but before the last fitting, so that you can try the gown on with your new lingerie and make sure that it all fits perfectly and doesn't show through. The trick is to match the right lingerie to the right dress. Don't worry about it not being sexy enough, you can change into your honeymoon lingerie later!

What lingerie is right for my dress shape?

Strapless bra

This style is essential for strapless gowns to give definition and shape, and to hold you in place. If you have a small bust, consider getting a padded bra; it will give you extra confidence and also help the gown stay in place.

Balconette bra

This is the perfect bra for a low scoop neck, Empire-line dress as it is low enough to be hidden, but offers support to enhance the cleavage. This also works well with a sexy column dress, as long as the bra has a seamless, plain design that won't be seen through the material.

Corset/basque

The most popular choice of brides-to-be, this style gives a bigger cleavage, nipped-in waist and flatter stomach. Make sure that it isn't too tight, so that you can breathe, and won't make you too busty.

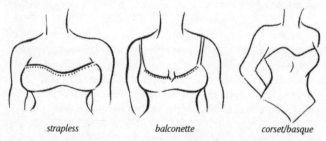

strapless   balconette   corset/basque

How can I make sure my lingerie is invisible?

No one wants a VPL or a bra strap hanging off a shoulder, particularly on their wedding day. One of the best ways to ensure that no one's going to know what you've got on under your dress is to invest in some nude-coloured lingerie. Even if it's not your normal colour, try it out because you'll be amazed at the difference it makes. It is also wise to opt for smooth, seam-free lingerie that won't show through. If you're having your dress made, you could ask the designer to add clips to the neckline of the dress to keep bra straps in place. Pants are better in a nude shade and choose a thong if you have a body-skimming dress.

If you're worried about the shape of your waist and bum, then try pants that have invisible panels to flatten the tummy and that lift the rear – it can change your shape instantly. If you want to reduce the size of your bust, then invest in a minimiser bra; alternatively, if you want to give it a boost, then there are some fantastic padded bras on the market.

Stockings and suspenders are best avoided until the first night or honeymoon, as they can be uncomfortable and will be visible if you are wearing a tight or sheer gown. If you are wearing a short gown, avoid the traditional white tights as they are unflattering; opt instead for a sheer nude shade with some shimmer. They will make your legs look tanned and slim. Ask your chief bridesmaid to carry a spare pair in her bag, just in case you have any snags.

> ☺ Go to a professional bra-fitter before you buy your new lingerie – two-thirds of women are wearing the wrong size bra!

Bridesmaids

The first obstacle to overcome when picking out the bridesmaid outfits is the question of who pays. These days it is usual for the bridesmaids to pay for their dresses themselves, and in the case of younger flower girls or pageboys, for their parents to pay. That said, if you're thinking Versace rather than Bhs, then you can't expect your friends to fork out so much and you will have to dig into your own pocket.

Can I tell them exactly what to wear?

The key is to be diplomatic. If one person insists on wearing a plunging neckline and short skirt and you envisaged your maids in chic high-neck column dresses, then compromise and search for something that is a little less formal but not too racy.

Everyone has horror stories of being made to wear the bridesmaid dress from hell, so keep this in the back of your mind when looking for outfits and keep consulting your friends about what they like to wear.

Don't feel that you have to buy from specialist bridesmaid gown companies. Your friends are doubtlessly going to want something glamorous that they can wear again, so head for stores that sell luxurious summer dresses and evening wear.

If you have bridesmaids with wildly different body shapes and heights, and you want them all to wear the same outfit, then pick a dress that looks good on the bridesmaid with the most difficult figure and it will undoubtedly look okay on the rest of the bridesmaids, albeit in different sizes.

You could stick to one colour, but use different dress styles to flatter various figures. Alternatively, if you have friends with very different skin tones, don't be afraid to mix the colours of the outfits. You could pick one hue and have it in darker and paler shades, or you could unify different dresses with a single colour accessory such as matching sashes.

> ☺ There is no rule that says all bridesmaids have to match. It can be far more fun to have a variety of shades.

If you are having younger maids, don't put them in anything too restricting or itchy, or you'll end up with grumpy-looking children on your wedding photos. Also, remember that they will get tired quickly, so don't give them any heavy baskets or bouquets to carry for long.

Can I tell my mum what to wear?

No, unless you want World War III to break out. Would you want to be told? I don't think so! Unless she specifically asks for your advice, she isn't going to appreciate you dictating what she can wear. However, what you can do is involve your mum and your mother-in-law in the wedding, giving them subtle hints about things like what your colour scheme will be and whether it's a very formal or informal affair, so they can build up a picture of how they should look.

It's also a good idea to take them along to a dress fitting if the store also sells mother-of-the-bride labels, because they may end up trying some outfits and you'll be able to give an honest opinion. Alternatively, offer to go shopping with them for their outfits. You could make it a fun day and also be directly involved in what they choose. At the end of the day, though, you love your mum for who she is and not what she wears and we're sure you'd rather have her there in a bright cerise pink two-piece than not at all!

Accessories

There are lots of bridal accessories around, but just remember that some of the most stylish looks are the simplest.

Should I wear a wedding veil?

Wedding veils were originally worn to protect the bride from evil spirits, and as a symbol of the bride's modesty and chastity. To most modern brides, however, it's a great accessory that looks fabulous with the wedding dress. Traditionally it was worn over the face, and then lifted after the vows had been exchanged. Alternatively, many modern brides choose to wear it back to frame their face from the start. If you do decide to wear a veil, there are several styles to choose from.

Cathedral

This is the longest style of veil, and usually extends at least 1.2 metres (4 feet) on to the floor. It's the best style to team with a gown with a long train, and is popular for traditional church weddings (see illustration on page 6 left).

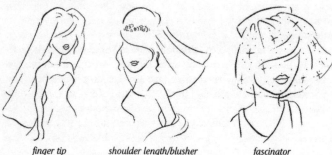

finger tip   *shoulder length/blusher*   *fascinator*

Full length
A full-length veil reaches to the floor and is ideally worn with a long, straight dress. It's a very dramatic length and ideal if you're having a formal, religious ceremony (see illustration on page 6 right).

Finger tip
A veil that reaches to hip level, this works best with a full skirt or 50s-style dress with nipped-in waist and flared skirt.

Shoulder length or blusher
This is the most popular style with modern brides, as it's usually the most flattering and complements all kinds of wedding gowns. It falls just below the shoulder and is sometimes tiered. It frames the face beautifully, is easy to attach and very light to wear.

Fascinator
A veil that only covers the face, this is a perfect choice for a civil ceremony. Wear it on its own, or attached to a hat for a really dramatic look. A fascinator works well with a short, modern outfit or trouser suit.

What should my veil be made of?
There are lots of fabrics to choose from, so try on a selection of veils to find which is the most comfortable and flattering for you. Lace is the traditional fabric of choice – think Grace Kelly when she tied the knot with Prince Rainier. However, although it is beautiful, lace can be very expensive and doesn't always work well with a modern outfit. Other options are tulle and synthetic net, which are stiffer and have more structure. Silk tulle is pricey but is very soft and looks fabulous.

If you're on a budget, have a go at making your own veil with a length of chiffon or tulle, simply draped over your hair and attached with flowers or clips – simple but elegant. Your veil could be embellished with pearls, sequins, beads and embroidery if you want to enhance it.

Should I wear a headdress?

There's a huge choice of headdress styles for modern brides, whether your hair is long or short, and the best way to discover what is the best style for you is to try them all.

Tiara

The ever-popular tiara is the number one choice of head wear for brides. What's more, the prices range from terrifying to low-budget, so there's something to suit everyone.

Alice band

A simple band worn towards the front of the head, this scrapes the hair away from the face for a fresh look. You could wear it plain and sophisticated, or try one that has been decorated with flowers to match your bouquet for a co-ordinated look.

Flowers

A chic look for modern brides, particularly those getting married abroad, is flowers in the hair. A popular style is the wreath, which is a band of flowers or foliage placed around the top of the head. This works particularly well with long, flowing hair with plenty of body. Other pretty floral options include rose buds pinned throughout your hair, which looks gorgeous on voluminous, curly styles. Alternatively, a single rose or lily tucked behind the ear is exquisite. Bear in mind that flowers tend to wilt on hot days, so you may want to consider using silk blooms.

Hat
If you are opting for a modern outfit, consider a hat for your head wear. Pillbox hats with a veil look particularly glamorous with a shift dress, while a wide, floppy brimmed hat can work well with a neat trouser suit – think Bianca Jagger.

Crown/coronet
Similar to the tiara, the crown or coronet is usually circular, sits on top of the head and is decorated with stones. This is a great accessory if you're going for a medieval or ballgown-style dress, but not advisable if you're wearing a sleek, straight outfit as it will detract attention from your gown.

> ☺ Take your headdress with you to a dress fitting to check that it complements your outfit. Also take it with you to the hairdressers before the day, so you can perfect your hairstyle.

How do I make my headdress secure?
It's essential that your headdress is pinned in place securely so that you won't be worrying about it during the day. Pop into your hairdressers for a consultation about the best way of securing your accessory. If you're doing it yourself, you'll need some Kirby grips to hook through your headpiece, and hair spray to help keep your hair in place. If you have very shiny or fine hair, it may be advisable for you to wash and blow dry your hair the day before the wedding rather than on the day itself, as your hair will then be less slippery on the day. Plaits are a great way of helping to keep everything in place, and are easy to attach things to.

Remember that people will be gazing at the back of your head during the ceremony, so make sure that you choose head wear that looks as good at the back as it does at the front.

> ☺ Have a quick dance around the room before you leave to check your head wear is secure – and release any tension!

Do I need a bag and gloves?

Most brides prefer to carry only a bouquet and ask their chief bridesmaid to hold a bag for essential items, like a mirror, lipstick or piece of chalk to white-out any stains on the wedding gown. Modern choices include floral bags by designers like Lulu Guinness, which double up as bouquet and handbag. If you would prefer to carry some small items yourself, consider asking for a pocket to be sewn into the seam of your gown.

Gloves can look very elegant, particularly with a ballgown-style dress, or long coat at a winter wedding. They are widely available from wedding stores, both three-quarter length and shorter to the wrist. Silk gloves are the more expensive choice, but cheaper options in satin look just as good. If you want to wear gloves during the ceremony, wear your engagement ring underneath, remove the gloves when you reach the groom and hand them to your chief bridesmaid or nearest member of the wedding party. Put them on again for the signing of the register, but remove them for the reception meal.

Shoes

What better excuse than your wedding day to flex the credit card and invest in some truly fabulous shoes? Before you get carried away with diamanté-encrusted stilettos with four-inch heels from Gina, it's important to remember to look out for style and comfort, because you're going to be on your feet a lot during your wedding day.

Should I wear high heels?

If you want to elongate your legs or you are wearing a shift dress, then you'll want high heels. If you aren't used to wearing them you're going to have to practise. Buy a cheap pair and walk around in them, otherwise, come the wedding day, you'll be tripping rather than walking up the aisle. If you prefer a more comfortable shoe or if you're worried about towering over your man, there are some fabulous flat options around. The all-time classic is the ballet pump, popularised by Audrey Hepburn, which looks pretty in pink and white and sets off any wedding gown. Tiny kitten heels are ideal to give you a little lift, and are easy to walk on.

I can't find shoes to match my outfit

There are companies, such as Rainbow, that will dye shoes to any shade you desire. You can also try shops that sell dance shoes, as they often offer a wedding-shoe dyeing service.

If you really can't find the right shoe for you, there are designers who offer a bespoke service, but expect to pay anything from £250 upwards. Don't forget to consider the time of year that you're getting married when choosing your shoes. A pretty pair of strappy sandals looks great in summer, but for a winter wedding outfit it's better to choose closed shoes, or even boots. If your shoes have smooth, flat soles and you're worried about slipping, simply scrub the bottom of the shoes with sandpaper to create a rougher surface. If you want a completely co-ordinated look, buy matching shoes and bag.

☺ Wear your shoes around the house for two weeks before the wedding so that they are worn in and comfortable.

Beauty

The key to looking great on the day is to choose a beauty regime well in advance, and to stick to it. If you fancy a totally new look, then start testing out ideas early on to find a look that you're comfortable with – and before you make any drastic changes remember that your hubby-to-be fell in love with you the way you are.

Should I go on a diet?

Everyone wants to look their best on their wedding day, and to some people this means losing weight and looking slimmer. A wedding date can be a great goal to lose a bit of weight but it has to be a sensible and realistic programme, such as 0.5 kg (1 lb) a week. Crash dieting is not recommended. Not only does it usually lead to unhealthy binge eating, but it may result in your dress not fitting on the day because you've lost so much weight. It will also leave you exhausted – which is the last thing that you want during the build-up to your lovely day.

The sensible alternative is to devise a healthy eating plan and gentle exercise routine. The minimum recommended amount is three sets of thirty minutes' exercise a week. You don't need to take out an expensive gym membership, as the exercise could be anything from brisk walking to riding a bike.

If the thought of cycling or jogging is your worst nightmare, consider yoga or pilates as a gentle alternative that will not only help to tone your body, but will also help you to learn calming techniques which you can use throughout the wedding day.

In terms of dietary requirements, your body needs fat, carbohydrates and protein to be healthy, so don't suddenly drop any of these just before the wedding. You can instantly make a difference to your diet by trimming any visible fat off foods like bacon and steak. This reduces your intake of harmful fat. Stick instead to polyunsaturated fats which are found in seeds and oily fish.

Eating more of the right things, like five portions of vegetables and fruit a day, will make an immediate difference. You may be tempted to cut out treats like biscuits and choc bars – don't; you'll only end up craving them and eating a whole packet. Instead, allow yourself a treat every once in a while.

☺ Don't weigh yourself twice a day, as not only can it be demoralising, it's also inaccurate, as your body constantly fluctuates due to its water content. To find out if you're really losing weight, step on the scales once a week.

The cheapest beauty and diet tip in the world is to drink two litres of water a day, as it not only helps to clear skin, but also makes you feel fuller and therefore less like snacking. It really does work, so start taking a bottle of water to work with you and you'll reap the benefits.

How can I get flawless skin for my wedding day?

Dermatologists recommend that you start a beauty routine for your skin up to six months before the wedding. The beginning of the routine should be to cleanse and moisturise every night. It's not rocket science, but it really will help to keep your skin flawless and radiant. Never try new products too close to the wedding day, especially if you have sensitive skin.

Cleanse

If you normally just use soap and water, experiment with different cleansers to see what is right for your skin and then stick to a day-and-night routine. In general, cream cleansers work well with drier skins, while water-based astringent cleansers work with oily skin. If you like the feeling after you've cleaned your face with water, there are lots of rinse-off cleansers on the market that are equally as good at wiping away dirt.

In addition, use an exfoliating scrub once a week to clear your pores, as blocked pores result in spots.

Moisturise

The right moisturiser can really make your skin glow, so it is well worth shopping around for the correct one for your skin type. If you have a T-zone, oily along the nose and forehead but dry cheeks, you may need to invest in two moisturisers.

Wear a good cream at night, as this is the time when the temperature of your skin rises and absorbs the moisturiser. For the daytime, invest in a cream with an SPF of at least 15, as the sun, along with smoking, is the biggest cause of premature lines and wrinkles.

Body care

For body maintenance, try switching to an exfoliating body scrub instead of your usual shower gel. You'll be amazed at how quickly your skin becomes smoother and feels firmer. This doesn't have to cost the earth; in fact, simple sea salt can make an effective scrub.

Enlist the help of your hubby-to-be and get him to give you some massages in the run-up to the wedding; not only will they help to relax you, they will also improve the skin as a massage gets the circulation going, helps shift cellulite and makes the body firmer. Remember to return the favour once in a while.

Don't forget to slather yourself in a good body moisturiser after a bath or shower, to prevent your skin drying out and becoming flaky.

> ☺ Finally, the best beauty treatment for your skin is eight glasses of water a day and seven hours' sleep a night.

Wedding-day beauty rescues
Spots
You wake up on the morning of your wedding and you've got a big spot on your normally flawless cheek. What do you do? Don't panic!

- Don't squeeze your spots, as this will only make them more prominent; instead, dab them with some alcohol, which helps to dry them out and reduce the redness and inflammation.
- You could also use a spot-buster or a couple of drops of Tea Tree oil.
- If you're hiring a make-up artist they will be able to work wonders with a good concealer and foundation.
- If you're doing your own make-up, it's worth investing in a good concealer well before the big day so that you have the comfort of knowing that you can cover any spots or blemishes.
- The key to disguising spots is blending. Apply concealer with your fingertips and work it into the skin in a dabbing motion; you may have to apply several times. Then apply foundation.
- There are ways of reducing the likelihood of spots in the run-up to the wedding. Don't have a facial 24 hours or less before the wedding day as this can cause an outbreak. Also, be well organised, as stress can have the same effect. Avoid bingeing on alcohol as the side effects can cause redness and poor skin.

Perspiration

If you're worried that being nervous will make you perspire a lot and that this will show through your wedding dress, talk to your GP about prescription antiperspirants that will put an end to the problem. There are also over-the-counter options, so ask your chemist about stronger-than-normal deodorants that will ensure you smell sweet all day.

Blushing bride

If you're the kind of girl who blushes a little too easily when all eyes are on you, there is help at hand. Snap up a skin-colour corrector – these usually have a green tint to cancel out the red. Worn under your foundation, this will ensure you walk down the aisle your usual colour.

White teeth

If you're loath to smile on your wedding photographs because you're less than happy with the colour of your teeth, why not ask your dentist about having them whitened? It's a fairly simple procedure that involves painting a solution on to the surface of the teeth before exposing them to a power laser for around three seconds per tooth. There are kits to whiten teeth at home, but this is not recommended.

Dark circles

If you've had some sleepless nights worrying about the wedding, then you may find that you end up with dark circles or bags under your eyes that wouldn't normally be there. A good way of reducing puffiness under the eyes is to place cooling cucumber slices on each closed lid for 10 minutes. It won't break the bank and it feels wonderful. To disguise dark circles, don't load on the foundation; instead, use a product specifically designed to lighten the skin and banish dark circles.

Shiny skin

If you're in the glare of the cameras and lights all day, you may be susceptible to the dreaded shiny forehead, cheeks and nose. If you're having a summer wedding, the heat, along with a swig or too of champagne, can make you look more Aunt Sally red cheeks than elegantly glowing. To achieve an instant shine-free finish, ask your chief bridesmaid to pop a powder compact or some blotting sheets in her bag, which you can discreetly dab on your face.

Eye sight

If you rely on glasses but don't want to wear them on your wedding day, chat to your optician about trying out some contact lenses. There is a wide variety now available on the market, including soft, daily disposables which you can simply chuck away at the end of the evening. Try them out several months before the wedding, as you have to build up tolerance so that your eye won't reject them.

If you already wear contact lenses, you could experiment with coloured lenses such as brown or blue for a striking look for the big day. If you're going to be wearing them all day and your eyes tend to dry out, ask your chief bridesmaid to pop some eye drops and a spare pair of lenses in her bag in case you have any mishaps.

Tanning

There's no denying that a white or ivory gown looks great against tanned skin. But that shouldn't mean you risk your health to get one, so no lying in the sun for months before your wedding – you'll look great now, but not in 20 years!

These days there are so many realistic fake tans on the market that there's no need to expose yourself to the dangers of sunbathing or the sun bed. You can either have it applied professionally at a beauty salon, which will take around an hour and cost from £35, or you can do the work yourself. If you do decide to apply your own fake tan, here are some tips to follow so that you avoid that orange, streaky look.

- Try out your chosen fake tan months before the wedding. This way you'll know that it's the right colour for you, and even if it isn't, it will have faded long before the big day.
- Before you apply, exfoliate thoroughly so the tan can be applied evenly, paying particular attention to rough bits of skin on the knees, elbows and feet.
- Moisturise your body well. This will help the application to be smooth and even.
- Only rub fake tan into areas where the sun would naturally brown your body. Have you ever seen someone with naturally tanned palms?
- Initially, keep the first layer light so you can see how it develops. Some fake tans can take up to six hours to reach full colour, so read the instructions carefully and don't keep applying more and more because you think it's having no effect. The ideal stage to reach is a light, natural tan that you can keep topping up each week in the run-up to the wedding.

Make-up

Practice makes perfect when it comes to your wedding-day make-up. Experiment with different looks well before the big day and don't be afraid to try things that aren't part of your usual make-up routine. Whether it's eyeliner or blusher – have some fun!

How do I achieve a flawless look?

Unless you have perfect skin, foundation is a make-up must and can help make your skin look perfect. So, even if you don't normally use foundation, your wedding would be a wise time to invest. There are some great products on the market that are light and can perfectly match your skin tone. Use one of these and smooth it in beyond your jawline to avoid ending up with tide marks underneath your chin.

> ☺ Ask for help at department-store beauty counters, where beauticians will be only too happy to help you try on lots of shades and types and show you how to apply them. These sessions are usually free.

Should I apply my own make-up?

There's no reason why you shouldn't apply your own make-up, particularly if you're on a budget and don't want to splash out on a make-up artist. If you've got a friend who is adept at applying it, you may want to recruit her to help come up with your look.

To get you started and feeling more confident, you might want to have a make-up lesson, which you could book at a beauty salon or department-store beauty counter, to find out how the professionals do it. Or you could buy a book on the art of make-up application for some hints and tips.

> ☺ Don't start experimenting with a new look on the day of the wedding.

It is a good idea to ask a friend to take Polaroids of the various looks that you try, so you can see what works well in photographs as well as in real life. It's not advisable to use make-up that's too trendy. You're going to be looking at your photos for years to come, and your make-up will quickly date if you go for a hot new look. Below are some useful guidelines to help you achieve an immaculate face.

Foundation

When picking a foundation, test it on your face rather than the back of your hand as the two are often different shades and will have different coverage. You are aiming for a perfect blend, and avoiding the orange face, jaw-line tide-mark problem.

These days there are some fantastic ranges which offer fabulous coverage for any skin type. If you're looking for a very light base, you could try a tinted moisturiser. For a heavier base and to cover flaws and disguise wrinkles, try a light-reflecting foundation. Brands such as Philosophy will actually mix together colours for you to create a perfect match for your skin tone.

Before you apply your foundation, you may want to rub a primer on your face and neck. This will help the foundation to stay on longer and stop it sliding in the heat.

The key to good coverage is in the blending, which you can do either with your fingers using upward strokes or with a make-up sponge. A good tip is to dampen the sponge slightly for a more even coverage.

> ☺ Apply concealer on any dark circles or blemishes and blot with powder. Then apply your foundation and seal with light powder to help your make-up stay put.

Lipstick
To achieve the perfect pout on your wedding day, you need to make the most of your luscious lips. If you're worried your lips are too thin, then take your lead from make-up artists who can make models go from thin to full in minutes. Simply cover your lips in foundation or concealer, trace the outline of your lips just outside their natural lip line and then fill in with a natural shade that blends right in to your new lip line. Don't use a different lip liner to your lipstick: not only does it look harsh and old-fashioned, it also makes your lips look thinner.

If you've got a fuller pout, make sure your lips are in tip-top condition and not chapped. Don't outline them as this will make them appear even larger. Bright colours will draw attention to your lips, nude colours will make them less of a prominent feature.

As you're going to be doing a lot of puckering up on your wedding day, you're going to want your lipstick to stay put. You can achieve this by applying one layer at a time, blotting your lips on a tissue, and then reapplying – repeat the process until you feel you've built up a good base. This layering will ensure that you have a perfect pout all day.

You might also want to invest in a stay-on lipstick, although these can sometimes dry out the lips. If you want to use a little gloss, apply it in the centre of the mouth as this makes lips look fuller.

Eye make-up
Even the coolest brides have been known to have a little cry (of happiness) at their wedding, so the first thing to invest in is some seriously good waterproof mascara.

When applying mascara, avoid panda eyes by popping a piece of tissue underneath each eye and dragging your mascara wand along the lower lashes. Then lower the lids and coat the top lashes in the same way. To complete the wide-eyed look, brush the mascara wand upwards underneath the top lashes. If you really want to extend the lashes, invest in an eyelash curler. Lots of women apply mascara first and then use the curler – don't, as this can cause your lashes to snap.

Your choice of eye shadow will depend on the colour of your eyes and how much you want to emphasise this area. It's best to decide whether you want to enhance your eyes or lips, but not both, unless you want to look like a vamp! A brush of neutral-coloured shadow, such as light brown, across the eyelid and then a lighter colour up to the brow gives depth and definition but looks very natural. If your eyes are quite close together and you want to make them appear more set apart, use a darker shade of shadow at the outer edge of the eye.

To define the eye clearly, you could use an eye-liner in brown or black. Pull the corner of the eye out to one side and close the lid, and with your other hand drag the liner from the inner eye to the outer edge of the eye in a clean sweep. It's tricky to apply, but once you've got it sussed it looks fabulous.

Blusher
To achieve a natural glow, smile and apply blusher to the apples of your cheeks and gently stroke the brush up towards your temples. Lightly brush the forehead and bridge of the nose for an all-over glow. Remember to blow off excess blusher from the brush before you start.

Make-up colours
Fair complexions are perfectly complemented by pastel shades like pink, beige and lavender. Don't feel that you have to stick to pink blusher and lips though – a brush of pink across the lids can look modern and lighten the eyes.

Olive complexions look fabulous with darker shades like berry on lips and as a blusher.

Dark eyes can be enhanced by smoky eye make-up, but don't overdo this sultry, evening-time look.

Black skin looks great with both very dark and very light shades. Consider using silver and gold on eyes for a modern look.

Eyebrows

According to make-up artists, the quickest way to change your look and improve your whole face is to shape your eyebrows. If you've never had a go at plucking your brows, but are tempted, don't start tweezing or waxing just before the wedding. Start by making an appointment with a professional. Eyebrow shaping costs from as little as £15, and then from £5 to tidy them up. You'll need to go at least three months before your wedding, enough time to allow for any correction growth and to make sure the shape is just right.

If you do want to tackle them yourself, there are some basic rules.

- Don't pluck away at one brow and then do the other, work between the two so that they match one another.
- Use a large mirror that shows your whole face. If you use a tiny hand-held mirror you won't get a true reflection of how your brows are looking in relation to the rest of your face.
- Shaping your eyebrows can act like an instant facelift, but plucking them into a thin line can add years on to your face, so go easy.
- Follow your eyebrows' natural line and pluck from beneath.

Avoiding mishaps

Wearing white or cream top-to-toe makes you a magnet for stains and smudges, so you're going to have to be extra vigilant when you're getting ready. Hang your dress up well away from where you're having your make-up and hair done.

On no account attempt to do things like paint your nails or apply some more lipstick after you've put your dress on; you'll be devastated if you have to walk down the aisle with a splodge of red nail varnish on your skirt. Instead, arrange to get your nails professionally done the day before; if you have a couple of coats it shouldn't chip.

If you can step into your dress, have your make-up done first and then clean your hands before you put it on. If your wedding dress has to be pulled on over your head, put it on first and then put on your make-up and have your hair styled, but only after you've covered the front of your dress in towels in case there are any mishaps.

If possible, only put your gown on at the last minute – the less you're wearing it, the less chance there is of you staining it.

☺ Give your chief bridesmaid your lipstick and nail varnish in case you need any touch-ups during the day.

Hair

One of the first things that people notice about you is your hair, so when all eyes are on you on your wedding day you'll want to know that it's extra special. This doesn't necessarily mean that you should suddenly go for a dazzling new colour or trendy cut. It means gorgeous, shiny hair that's in fabulous condition.

What's the ideal wedding hairstyle?

There's isn't one wedding hairstyle that suits everyone, so start thinking about your locks well before the big day, so that you can experiment with looks. When choosing your style, it's important to think about what you'll be wearing and what sort of look you want to achieve. For a more formal, traditional wedding, brides often choose an 'up' style which looks fabulous with a tiara and makes the neck look long and graceful.

Many women feel under pressure to grow their hair for their wedding day, but if you are happy with a short style and have had it that way for some time, it's probably because that's what suits you best.

If you do long for lengthy tresses, however, and know that your hair won't grow in time, consider having hair extensions.

If you're going to experiment with colour, either darker or lighter, it is best to begin up to six months in advance to allow regrowth if you're not happy. Also, ask for semi-permanent colour so that you know it will fade back to your natural colour.

How can I make my hair look healthier?

To start getting your hair in good condition for the big day, ensure you get the ends of your hair trimmed every six to eight weeks to get rid of split ends, and start using a deep intensive conditioner once a week.

It helps to have as healthy a diet as possible in the build-up to the wedding, to get both your skin and hair in great condition. In particular, try to get a good dose of fatty acids, found in vegetable oils, oily fish and nuts, which will help your hair to shine. For an artificial boost for lack-lustre hair, try treatment shampoos, conditioners and hot oils which should help it to spring back to life. If you're worried about frizzy or unmanageable hair, invest in some straighteners and serums to leave your hair silky-smooth and shiny.

For very fine, flat hair, use volumising shampoo and conditioner to give your hair more bounce and condition.

If you are styling your own hair and want to achieve a salon-perfect finish, follow these steps:

- Wash and towel-dry your hair, then comb it to get rid of tangles.
- Spray on a product for protecting the hair during blow drying.
- Divide the hair into sections and pin back.
- Start by drying the underneath sections.
- Use an anti-static flat paddle brush for straight hair or a round brush for more volume.
- Finish off with shine serum to keep any stray hairs in place.

How can I get rid of unwanted hair?

You'll want to be silky smooth all over for your wedding night and honeymoon, and the quickest and cheapest method is to use a razor. There are some razors that have a strip at the top of each blade that releases botanical oils, vitamin E and aloe to moisturise the skin.

If you don't want to shave every day, you could opt for a wax. You can buy home waxing kits or you may prefer to go to a beauty salon. Be warned, waxing can be painful and can (temporarily) leave you with red marks, so it's not something to be doing on the morning of your wedding.

Other hair removal methods include depilatory creams and mousses.

For permanent hair removal, you can visit a beauty clinic that offers electrolysis or laser hair removal. The hair is killed at its root, but you are likely to have a couple of finer regrowths before the hair is permanently destroyed, so if you want this treatment, you've got to plan it at least six months before the wedding. It's vital that this is carried out by a trained professional or it could result in scarring.

Nails

Even if you usually don't bother about your nails, your wedding day is one time when you're going to want to have perfect nails – hands and toes! You'll be shaking guests' hands all day and your hands will be on lots of the key photographs, such as when you're cutting the cake.

Where should I go for a manicure?

You could visit a nail bar, beauty counter or beautician. A manicure will cost from about £15. Alternatively, if you've got a friend who is great at applying nail varnish, then ask her around to experiment with colours and ask her to shape your nails.

You don't have to opt for a colour, as clear nail varnish works well. You could have a French manicure and have the tips of your nails whitened. If you bite your nails or can't grown them very long, you could always look at getting nail extensions for your wedding day. A good set professionally applied costs from £50.

Can I do my nails myself?

With practice, you can do your own manicure. Follow these simple steps.

- Wash your hands thoroughly and then apply hand cream.
- Gently push back your cuticles using an orange stick.
- Shape your nails using a nail file rather than scissors, and file in one direction rather than using a seesaw action as this weakens the nail and can cause splitting.
- Buff the nails for a polished, smooth surface.
- Apply a base coat to strengthen the nail and create an even surface.
- Apply your chosen varnish by placing the brush in the centre of the

nail and then pushing out to the sides. Be careful not to touch the cuticles.

- Apply a couple of coats and don't come into contact with anything while your nails are drying as the varnish will smudge easily.

What's an ideal perfume for my wedding day?

Your scent choice depends entirely on whether you prefer light or musky perfumes. If you prefer heavier scents you could go for a classic like Chanel No 5, for lighter perfumes try Contradiction by Calvin Klein or Beautiful by Estée Lauder. You could wear something symbolic, such as Happy by Clinique or Romance by Ralph Lauren.

If you are worried that your perfume will wear off after a couple of hours, invest in some bath and body products in the same scent to build up layers of the perfume.

> ☺ Before you step into your dress, spray your eau de toilette up and down just in front of you and then walk though it. Do this twice so that you're enveloped in a fine mist from head to toe.

Should I hire a professional?

If you want to enlist the help of a professional hair or make-up artist, then pick wisely. Always interview them before you book them, to make sure that you like their style. You also want someone you can trust and who makes you feel relaxed.

Ask to see their work, not just studio shots, but real-life weddings to see that they can work wonders on the public as well as models. Check that it will be them and not an assistant who will be producing your look on the big day, and also find out whether they are going to be able to come to your house or whether you'll have to travel to them on the day of the wedding. Check prices as they usually start from £100.

Once you're happy and you've booked them, have a few meetings with them in the run-up to the wedding to try out different looks and styles. You don't want them arriving at your house on the day of the wedding and creating a look that you're not prepared for. It helps to have an idea in your mind about the look you want, so try cutting out pictures of hair and make-up that you want to emulate.

> ☺ In the week before the wedding day, telephone your hair and make-up artists to confirm times and dates with them.

How can I stay relaxed?

Planning a wedding can be one of the most fun and satisfying things you can do in life, but it can also be extremely stressful. The last thing that you want to do is to make yourself ill in the run-up to the big day, so it's vital that you stay as relaxed and calm as possible even when it's drawing close.

Why not plan a spa day with your bridesmaids the week before your wedding and treat yourself to a relaxing massage. Take up yoga or pilates which will help to calm you down and to tone your body. Boost your immune system by eating plenty of healthy fruit and vegetables, as stress can leave you feeling run-down and tired. Take extra zinc and vitamin C which can help fight off colds: the last thing you want is watery eyes and a blocked-up nose.

☺ The night before the wedding, indulge in a relaxing bath. Sprinkle in calm-inducing aromatherapy oils, such as lavender, and you'll be out like a light when your head hits the pillow.

What to take on the day

The essential items you need to pop into a bag to give to your chief bridesmaid are:

- compact powder and mirror
- miniature lipstick
- concealer
- eye drops
- tissues
- miniature scent bottle
- miniature nail file
- hairbrush
- white chalk to cover any marks on your dress.

Chapter 6
Flowers

Buying flowers always feels like a wonderful luxury, but for your wedding day flowers are essential. Whether you are lavishly filling a room with 400 pink roses or carrying a simple bouquet of daisies, your flowers will mirror the colour, tone and beauty of your big day.

Seasonal flowers

Florists are able to get hold of most flowers pretty much all year round. The price can go up enormously, however, if they are out of season, so it's worth checking out what beautiful blooms are on the market for the time of year when you are planning to get hitched. This list will give you a rough idea of when certain popular flowers start to become more easily available.

- **January:** Early bulb flowers, heather, hellebore.
- **February:** Amaryllis, iris, primula, reticulata, violets.
- **March:** Bluebells, camellias, cherry blossom, forget-me-knots, hyacinth.
- **April:** Crocus, daffodils, lily of the valley, poppies, ranunculus, tulips.
- **May:** Cornflowers, marguerites, peonies, stock.
- **June:** Bouvardia, delphiniums, gardenia, gypsophila, sweet william.

- **July:** Allium, chrysanthemum, marguerites, nigella, phlox, roses.
- **August:** Aster, gladioli, jasmine, larkspur, poppies, sweet peas.
- **September:** Dahlia, lavender, love-lies-bleeding, nerines, ornamental cabbage, late sunflowers.
- **October:** Astilbe, celosia, cockscomb, hypericum, pinks.
- **November:** Daffodils, hyacinth, snowdrops.
- **December:** Dutch hyacinth, passion flower, narcissus.
- **All year:** Carnations, freesia, gerberas, lilies, orchids.

Choosing a florist

Some of the best ways to find a florist are:

- asking for recommendations from friends whose wedding flowers you admired
- looking through wedding magazines for styles that you like
- asking staff at your wedding venue for contacts
- looking on the internet or in Yellow Pages for florists in your area.

When you've chosen some reputable florists, make appointments and meet up for face-to-face chats about what you want. Try to see at least three, to give you a choice and to allow you to compare prices. Always ask to see a portfolio of work, including real-life weddings, so that you can see whether you like their work.

Things to discuss before hiring a florist include your budget and the location of the wedding.

- Find out if the florist knows your wedding venue, and if they don't, suggest that they pay a visit so that they can estimate how many flowers you'll need and where they should go.
- If you decide to book a florist, ask for an estimate first before signing anything, so that if it's far too expensive you have time to rethink.

- Don't be talked into elaborate, expensive arrangements when you know you simply haven't got the budget, as it'll only lead to trouble further down the line. Bear in mind that the more embellishments and props you want, like crystals, beads, urns and feathers, the more expensive your flower bill will be.
- If it is too expensive, don't despair, a good florist will be able to help you cut down on costs, by using less expensive flowers, for example.
- The majority of florists will require a deposit of between 25 and 50 per cent, so be sure to have that available to pay upfront.

It's useful to have an idea about colour schemes and also types of flowers that you like as it will help the florist to come up with suitable designs. If you can, take along fabric swatches of your dress and your attendants' outfits. It's also helpful for the florist to know how you will be decorating your reception, such as individual table centrepieces or a floral arch on arrival.

Finally, give your florist a list of names for the wedding party and what flowers they'll be wearing or holding. This way they'll know exactly how many people they've got to create designs for and in what colours.

Colour schemes

The most popular colour choices for wedding flowers are pink, white and lavender, but modern brides are also liable to opt for something eye catching like cerise pink roses or orange gerberas. While some brides prefer their flowers to co-ordinate perfectly, others may want their flowers to stand out and make them the colour injection of the day. There is also the decision of whether to mix flowers, or to stick to the same shade and flower throughout. The choice is yours!

Light creams, whites and ivories

Paler flowers are usually the most fragrant blooms, so if you want your bouquet or centrepieces to smell as good as they look, go for a white-out. Popular flowers include tuberose, ranunculus, lilies, white hellebore, amaryllis, dendrobium, orchids, euphorbia fulgens and tulips.

Pastel pinks, blues and lilacs

Whether pretty pastels or vibrant shots of colour, these shades are excellent on their own or mixed together. Lilac is a popular colour for modern weddings, while pink is a timeless classic that always works on romantic occasions. Recommended flowers in this category include anemones, hydrangeas, roses, peonies, celosia, lilac and pink nerines.

Deep reds, yellows, oranges and purples

For the contemporary bride who wants to make a real impact, deep, sensuous colours are an absolute must. These darker shades work wonderfully well against cream and white back-drops, so are ideal in bouquets and on white table cloths as reception centrepieces. Must-haves in these colours include roses, gerbera, cymbidium, arum lily, amaryllis, bouvardia and tropical flowers like anthurium – ideal for a wedding abroad.

What should my bouquet look like?

A bride's bouquet says as much about her as her dress does. Are you a neat, posy kind of bride or a flamboyant, trailing shower bouquet type? Your personal taste will also need to take into account your colour schemes, scents, the theme of the day and, most important of all, the style of your dress.

Style-wise, a large, trailing bouquet tends to look better with a ballgown-style of dress, while a slim-fit bias-cut gown needs something sleeker, such as a sheath of lilies or a tightly packed bunch of roses. If you're opting for a shift dress or a suit, you can get away with something a little funkier, like a cute handbag with flowers attached. Don't forget to ask about foliage as it frames a bouquet perfectly. Popular greens include bear grass, ivy and eucalyptus.

If you want a more innovative design, consider asking your florist to thread sequins, beads, crystals or pieces of soft fabric through your bouquet.

The most popular wedding flowers, such as arum lilies and lily of the valley are also the most expensive. If you want trendy blooms for less, go for daisy-like September flowers or sweet peas.

A popular idea used in the United States is to ask your florist to tie three bunches of flowers loosely together to form your bouquet. When you walk down the aisle after the ceremony, you can hand one to your mum and one to his, keeping the third for yourself.

☺ If you want to keep your bouquet after the wedding, consider having it dried professionally. Otherwise, you can press a few petals and keep them in your wedding album.

Flower talk

Many brides also choose a flower that has a special meaning.

- **Amaryllis:** Splendid beauty or pride.
- **Chrysanthemum:** Joy.

- **Freesia:** Innocence.
- **Lavender:** Devotion.
- **Lily:** Forever in love.
- **Narcissus:** Self-esteem.
- **Peony:** Most beautiful.
- **Rose:** Symbol of love.
- **Sweet pea:** Delicate pleasures.
- **Sunflower:** Adulation.
- **Tulip:** Declaration of love.

And for the rest of the wedding party ...

Bridesmaids

The key to your attendants' flowers is to keep them small and simple. The bride should have the biggest bouquet and it should also set the tone for the rest of the flowers.

Use the same types of flowers or colours that are in your own bouquet for co-ordination. If you don't want all their flowers to be identical, why not select one bloom from your bouquet and use it in a different shade for each maid? Alternatively, choose flowers that will match their outfits.

You may want your chief bridesmaid to have a different or larger bouquet to make her stand out from the other attendants. If you are having young flower maids, choose something light and easy for them to carry, such as a tiny posy or basket filled with petals.

If you want to be a little more inventive, other fun floral options for all your maids include flowers in their hair, floral chokers and corsages, pomanders, tiaras with flowers attached and floral handbags.

A sweet touch is to ask your florist to attach handwritten notes to each of the attendants' posies telling them what a great friend they are – just make sure that your chief bridesmaid has some tissues on hand!

> ☺ Ask pageboys to carry a box of petals to throw as confetti if they don't want to carry a posy of flowers.

The men

If you want the male members of the wedding party to wear classic buttonholes, go for a single rose with a little foliage to frame it. If you like everything to be ordered, then you may want the men at your wedding to be wearing boutonnières that are in sync with your own bouquet. For more contemporary buttonholes, use single, striking flowers such as cymbidium, amaryllis or an orchid lily. As with every aspect of your wedding, of course, you can choose whatever you like.

The male members of the wedding party who usually need buttonholes are the groom, ushers, best man and fathers of the bride and groom. Remember to give the chief usher extra pins on the day in case people need help securing them.

> ☺ Order two extra buttonholes for the day, as there's bound to be one that gets accidentally dropped or lost.

The mums

Mums certainly won't want to be left out of the proceedings, so ask in advance if they will want to wear a corsage on the day. Usually larger than a buttonhole, corsages are pinned to lapels or the chest and are a fabulous way of making mums feel special and part of the proceedings.

As with your bridesmaids, consult them about colours as flowers matching your bouquet may clash with their wedding outfit.

☺ If your mum is worried that pinning a corsage to her outfit may tear the fabric, suggest that she wears it around her wrist.

Ceremony flowers

For a church wedding you'll need to check with the minister exactly where you are allowed to put flowers. When you've been given the green light to access all areas, make a list of places that you want to decorate.

These usually include the entrance gate, porch, pew-ends, pillars, pulpit, altar and any windowsills. Flower arches can look wonderful; the best places for these are the outer and inner entrances and the aisle. If you are having a candle-lit ceremony, it can look enchanting to place flowers or strew petals around the base of the candle holders.

Flowers can be a wonderful way of disguising any musty church smells that may be around, so why not choose blooms like lilies, phlox and roses which will emit a heavenly scent into the air. Decorating a church can prove hugely expensive, so if you are on a tight budget, just concentrate on the areas that need brightening up, like the entrance and the ends of the pews.

For civil ceremonies in a licensed venue you will also need to check first with the management to find out where you are able to place flowers; in most cases this will be pretty much anywhere. If you're worried that the ceremony room is dull or lacking colour, flowers are the ideal way to liven things up. Attach them to chair backs, place them on windowsills and place arches around doorways.

If you're having your ceremony at a register office, your floral decorations are going to be limited. It is unlikely that you will be able to decorate windows and seats, as there will be other marriages taking place in the same room on the same day. Instead, give members of the wedding party flowers to hold.

A wonderful way to incorporate flowers into the ceremony is for guests to throw petals over the bride and groom as they leave the church or venue. Arrange for bags to be handed out or have baskets of petals waiting at the exit. Alternatively, pageboys and flower girls could sprinkle petals in the path of the bride and groom as they depart.

Reception flowers

Whether you're having informal canapés and champagne or a sit-down three-course meal for your reception, you're going to want some flowers to brighten up the proceedings. Reception flowers don't have to be expensive, and are a great way of beautifying otherwise ordinary objects such as chairs and napkins.

Centrepieces

Your table centrepieces are one of the most important floral displays, because they should bring together the look of your whole reception.

If you're having a sit-down wedding breakfast, you need a centrepiece for the middle of every table. Your choice may be inspired by your ceremony flowers, or you may want to co-ordinate with the colours and flowers from your bouquet.

Remember, it needn't be a huge display. It's currently popular to have single blooms in individual vases, which looks fabulous and keeps costs down. Another simple centrepiece which is very effective is floating candles and flower heads in a glass bowl.

Candles are also useful if you've got empty space to fill on your reception tables and are on a budget. Use votive candles surrounded by rose petals as centrepieces. Not only is this economical, it looks fabulous and will bathe the room in soft, romantic lighting.

> ☺ Whatever centrepieces you decide to have, it's important that they are arranged above or below eye level, otherwise guests won't be able to see each other across the table.

Place decorations and favours

If you're having a sit-down reception, you could seat your guests with the usual name cards, or you could go for a funky floral option instead. Some of the best designs are also the most simple – what about a couple of flowers in a shot glass with a ribbon and name tag tied around it? Or try a single rose stem laid at each setting with the guest's name written in metallic pen on a leaf. Pop a single flower into folded napkins, or tie foliage around the napkins. If you want floral favours instead of sweets for your guests, ask your florist to fill tiny terracotta pots with flowers and, with a ribbon, tie on a card showing the date of the wedding.

Chair decorations

Flower arrangements attached to the backs of chairs look exquisite and can really lift the look of the whole reception. If you need inspiration for chair backs, start with your bouquet or table centrepieces. Is there a particular colour or bloom in them that you want to use? A mini version of your bouquet tied to chairs with ribbon is a sweet option – guests could even take them home.

Another simple idea is to tie a couple of flowers together and attach them to the top of each chair, alternating the colours for male and female guests. If you want something more adventurous, discuss a more elaborate display with your florist. Fun ideas include wreaths, heart-shaped displays and garlands of petals to drape over the back of the chair. If you're on a tight budget, why not get chair backs for the wedding table only, or just the bride's and groom's chairs.

Do be sure to check the colour of the reception chairs before commissioning your florist: you don't want to arrive on the day and find that the hire chairs have bright red seat covers and your floral chair backs are a clashing cerise pink. Also remember to keep it subtle – you don't want enormous chair backs swamping the tables. And give your florist lots of prior warning.

Something extra

There's no reason why you have to stick to tables and chairs, Flowers can enhance any object, so if you've got the budget, check out other areas you can brighten up. Canapé or buffet trays can be made chic with single flower heads or petals. You could even serve up edible flowers in salads.

The coolest way to incorporate flowers into your reception party is to freeze individual rose petals in ice cubes. If your catering company can't make them, you could always call in the help of specialist ice companies, or even have a go at making them yourself.

Use fresh flowers to lighten up dark corners; scatter petals over the floor of your reception, or if money's no object, how about making a pathway of rose petals to the top table?

Chapter 7
Photography

Once the excitement of the big day is over, you have memories – and hopefully an album full of fabulous photographs that you can treasure forever.

Choosing the right photographer

Great photographs are the best memento you can have of your big day so you'll want to ensure that your photographer is picture-perfect.

If you're thinking about cutting back on photography and asking a friend to do it, think again. A professional photographer is going to be able to record your special day in style because they have the technical skill and experience to capture the moment. Good wedding photographers can be booked up a year in advance, so it's vital that you start searching as soon as possible in order to get the right photographer for you.

When you start shopping around for your dream snapper, you'll become aware of the huge differences in style, quality and prices available. It helps if you have set your budget early, so you know exactly how much you have to spend. It is also helpful to establish what style of photography you prefer. To find a good selection of photographers, ask friends for recommendations and try the internet and Yellow Pages for details of photographers in your area. Other good sources of inspiration are wedding magazines and wedding fayres.

Top tips to help you choose

1 Make appointments and ask to see a portfolio, including at least 15 shots from the same wedding to check that the high standards are consistent throughout the day.

2 Make sure that the photographer is used to taking shots at weddings, rather than portraits in a studio environment. Taking photographs of groups outside is very skilful and the photographer needs to be used to this.

3 First impressions count, and if you don't feel comfortable or able to talk about what you want, then carry on shopping around. You're going to be spending a lot of time with this person and trusting them with your precious photographs, so choose wisely.

4 Know from the start exactly what you are going to be getting for your money – most couples spend around five per cent of their budget on photography – and check what you will be getting so that no extra costs creep in. Look at travelling expenses, film and processing and prices for different types of prints.

5 A good wedding photographer will organise a pre-wedding meeting so that you can discuss the day in full. Look through their books and point out pictures that you particularly like or dislike so they will have an idea of what you want. However, remember that no two wedding photographs can ever be exactly the same; what you wear, the weather and the setting will all make yours unique.

6 It's a great idea for the photographer to visit the venue if they're not already familiar with it. This way they can get a good idea about backdrops and give you advice about where to pose.

7 Not all photographers stay for the reception, so ask in advance if they will stay and if there is any extra cost. Agree their leaving time and add the shots to your checklist.

Photography checklist

You may be happy for your photographer to snap away throughout the day and then compile a selection of shots from which you can choose. If you want to be more in control of things, it's a good idea to come up with your own list of must-have shots; this is the best way to guarantee that you won't be disappointed with your wedding pictures.

This list will give you some idea of the most traditional shots, although it's very much up to you. The idea of having a photograph taken while putting on make-up fills some brides with complete horror!

Some ministers only allow a limited number of shots to be taken inside the church, so do check first. You may also have a limit on the total number, so narrow down your list to the shots you really want.

Pre-ceremony shots

- Bride in dress
- Bride with parents
- Bride with family
- Bride with maid of honour
- Bride with bridesmaids
- Bride putting on make-up
- Bride and father getting into car
- Bride's parents

Ceremony shots

- Guests outside the venue
- Bride and father leaving car
- Bride and father entering venue
- Ushers escorting guests
- Soloist or organist
- Groom and best man
- Bride and father walking down aisle
- Couple exchanging vows
- Guests at service
- Ring exchange
- Signing
- Bridesmaids coming down aisle
- Couple coming down aisle
- Couple outside venue
- Couple getting into car

Pre-reception shots
- Bride
- Bride and maid of honour
- Bride and bridesmaids
- Bride, maid of honour and bridesmaids
- Groom
- Groom and best man
- Groom, best man and ushers
- Bride, best man and ushers
- Couple with all attendants
- Bride and her parents
- Bride with groom's parents
- Bride with mothers
- Bride with fathers
- Bride with all parents
- Groom and his parents
- Groom with bride's parents
- Groom with mothers
- Groom with fathers
- Groom with all parents
- Groom and bridesmaids
- Couple with bride's parents
- Couple with groom's parents
- Couple with mothers
- Couple with fathers
- Couple with all parents
- Couple with whole wedding party

Reception
- Couple arriving
- Couple going into reception
- Receiving line
- Table shots
- Cake shot
- Couple cutting cake
- Couple toasting
- Speeches
- Musicians
- Couple's first dance
- Bride and father dancing
- Throwing and catching bouquet
- Couple getting into car
- Rear of car as it departs
- Group shot of guests

Styles of photography

Wedding photography is no longer about an album full of formal, posed shots.

The emphasis now is far more on individuality and making your photographs a unique record of your big day. Pictures of the bride and groom and wedding party are essential, but so too are shots that capture your wedding style, whether it's a shot of your gorgeous wedding shoes or a snap of a wonderful place setting.

Traditional

Traditional doesn't have to mean old-fashioned. In terms of wedding photography it means beautiful, posed shots. Although this style is not as popular as it used to be, it is still the best way of recording exactly who was at the wedding and making sure everyone is included. These shots are also ideal to send to relatives who want a picture of the day. However, posed shots do take more time to arrange so bear this in mind when planning your reception – there's nothing worse than wedding guests being forced to wait around and starting to moan about the amount of time it takes to photograph the wedding party.

Reportage

This journalistic style is the most popular technique with modern brides. It has a storybook feel that is also very natural. It is largely based around impromptu moments, such as the groom laughing at a joke made by the best man or the bride hugging her maid of honour. The benefits of this type of photography are that the day can flow without interruptions. All smiles are guaranteed to be 100 per cent natural and when done well, these photographs can capture moments you weren't even aware were happening, which can be great keepsakes of the big day. However, it can only work well if the photographer is very discreet and highly skilled, so check that they are experienced in this field. Ask your wedding venue if they will allow your photographer to take shots during the ceremony and signing of the register so that the style can continue to be relaxed and not posed throughout.

> ☺ If you want natural shots, why not put disposable cameras on each reception table and invite guests to get snapping.

Colour or black and white?

Black and white is currently enjoying a huge revival in wedding photography. Not only does it instantly make details look classic and stylish, it is also very flattering. However, if you want to capture the vibrancy of your wedding, then you'll want to have some colour shots in there. The answer is to ask your photographer to take a selection in colour, and black and white, using separate cameras. This way you get some trendy black and white shots, but also don't miss out on essential colour details like your bouquet and the cake. If you really want a timeless feel to your wedding photographs, you could also consider requesting some in sepia. The faded, soft tones that this style gives can make a romantic addition to your album and are bound to be loved by the older members of your wedding party.

Another way of injecting some colour in black and white and sepia shots is to have some details in the photographs colour tinted by hand. The effect can be very striking, but don't overdo it.

How can I look fabulous in photographs?

Why is it that when celebrities are photographed they always look fabulous? Well, believe it or not, it's not just great hair and make-up, it's also because they know all the tricks of the trade when it comes to posing.

Everyone has experienced the disappointment of getting holiday snaps back and looking at a succession of unflattering photographs that reveal double chins and chubby upper arms that you never even knew you had. This is not what you want on your wedding photographs. A good photographer should make you feel at ease and help you to find the best look, but here are a few hints to help you on the big day.

- Remember to smile. A vibrant smile lights up any photograph and you'll look instantly radiant.
- Make sure that you are being photographed from above or at eye level, never below, as this will make you appear larger and reveal any unsightly double chins.
- Turn your body to a 45-degree angle to the photographer. It sounds strange, but if you face the camera straight on it makes you look two dimensional and broader, and adds weight. To look even slimmer, stand or sit at an angle, then turn your head and shoulders to face the camera.
- Check your make-up. You're not being vain, you just want to look perfect. Blot oily skin, put on lip gloss for plumper lips, check your mascara for panda eyes and brush your hair away from your face.
- Don't press your arms into your sides, as it makes even the thinnest arms look flabby. Instead, hold them slightly away from the body and bend them slightly. If you're standing next to someone, put an arm round their waist, so your arms aren't just hanging by your side.

- Drop your shoulders and push them back. This instantly makes your bust look more pert and prominent, extends your neck and makes you appear taller.
- Avoid staring into bright sunshine as it makes you screw up your eyes and creates black shadows over the eye sockets.
- Take Polaroids of some poses before the wedding and see which ones you like best. Then practise them.
- Ask your maid of honour to carry a little bag of emergency items like lipstick, concealer, compact powder and mirror, tissues and hairbrush in case any touch-ups are needed during the day.

Do we need a video of the wedding?

A video is a fun way of remembering your wedding day. You can sit down with a glass of wine when you get back from your honeymoon and relive your perfect day. It's an ideal gift for relatives and friends who couldn't make the wedding day, and is also a great way to find out what went on at your own wedding! The day tends to whiz by so quickly, and there are so many people to meet and greet, that you can sometimes miss out on what's going on elsewhere in the venue. But, again, there are no rules when it comes to organising your wedding. If you don't want to have the day captured on film, you don't have to.

Where do we find a videographer?

Some couples are happy for a friend to record the event with a home camcorder. While new technology means that the standard of handheld cameras is now very high, bear in mind that the filming, editing and picture quality is unlikely to be of as high a standard as that of a professional. If your videographer doesn't have microphones that can pick up sounds from some distance, then you'll lose the clarity of the vows and speeches. It also means that whoever is videoing the proceedings is missing out on actually watching one of the happiest days of your life.

If you want your wedding to be professionally videoed, finding a videographer is similar to picking a photographer. You need to ensure that they are professional, so check out members of the Association of Professional Videomakers and the Institute of Videography. Expect to pay from £500 upwards, with exceptionally good videographers charging £700 plus.

What should we be looking for?

Ask whether the videographer has had plenty of experience videoing weddings and ask to see lots of examples of his or her work. Simply being a cameraman or -woman doesn't mean that someone is going to be great at making a wedding video.

Weddings are exceptionally difficult to capture on film. They are often fast-moving, with lots of things going on at once and then lots of 'dead' time when not much is happening, such as when the photographs are being taken. There are also difficult lighting situations, such as dark churches and then bright sunshine outside, and poor acoustics.

When looking at examples of the videographer's previous work there are some key things to look out for:

- unevenness of colour
- out-of-focus images
- boring camera angles
- distorted sound
- camera shakes

Be sure to watch the demo tapes several times, because what may seem like a seamless piece of film first off, may expose more faults after you've watched it a couple of times.

What should we be asking for?

If you do want to go ahead and book your videographer, you'll need to discuss with them exactly what you want from the package. Start by discussing how your video will be edited. Some videographers will try to cut costs and save time by editing in-camera, which means they will only shoot the basics, such as ceremony, speeches, cake cutting and first dance. While this may be adequate, bear in mind that some of the funniest and most touching moments may well be spontaneous parts of the day, which a good videographer will be able to catch, even if it means shooting extra footage.

Establish how long you would like the videographer to be filming for, and suggest that he or she visits the venue to find out exactly where it is permitted to film without intruding on the ceremony or reception. Negotiate what you will be getting for your money from the start, such as how many copies you will receive.

You will also have to pick your style of video. Some couples are happy with a simple record of the day, without sound-tracks and lots of fancy editing. If you want something a bit more polished, though, ask about what is available to enhance the video, such as a voice-over or a sound-track. You also have to choose the kind of filming technique you want. A fly-on-the-wall documentary will capture all of the fun moments of your big day without any intrusion, but it can also be amusing to have some light-hearted interviews in the footage so that friends' and families' thoughts are recorded.

New technology

You don't have to take a science degree to pick your photographic formats, but it is worth checking out some of the latest advancements in photographic technology as it can provide some fun and funky alternatives to the usual shots.

Photographs taken on a digital camera are kept on storage cards which can be downloaded on to a computer and copied to floppy disks or CD. This fantastic development means that at the click of a button you can send images of your wedding via e-mail to friends and family around the world. Modern brides may also want to set up a web site that friends can access with details of the wedding and reception, and the images can easily be downloaded on to it. It is also a great back-up in case your wedding album or negatives become lost or damaged.

One of the most exciting new advancements for weddings is the web cam, which allows you to record the exchanging of vows and send it live via the world wide web to family and friends all over the world. There are also companies such as Yourcast TV which will put together a wed-cast package of video, commentary, graphics and picture stills and then invite anyone who couldn't make it to the wedding to log on to your wed-cast using a password which will have been e-mailed to them previously.

Digitial imaging is another great development in photography. It allows pictures that have been downloaded on to the computer to be altered. This means that colours can be enhanced and any unwanted background details can be wiped out. More importantly for brides everywhere, it means that skin blemishes and fly-away hair can disappear in an instant.

Chapter 8
The Reception

This it the part you're really looking forward to (apart from exchanging vows, of course!). The serious bit is over, you're Mr and Mrs and it is time to put on your dancing shoes and enjoy the party. The only trouble is, you've got to organise it first ...

Venues

If you're not having the ceremony and reception in the same venue, then you're going to have to hire somewhere for the party. Hotels and marquees are among the most popular choices, but if you fancy something a little more unusual there are lots of exciting options to consider, including clubs, castles, football grounds and country mansions.

Choosing the venue

Wedding venues are booked up notoriously early, so you do need to start hunting out your ideal venue as soon as possible. Good sources of information are wedding magazines, venue books, such as *Noble's Party Venues Guide,* the Yellow Pages, friends' recommendations and the internet.

Your first consideration is the distance between the ceremony and the reception venue. If the two are more than 30 minutes apart, then it may be worth laying on minibuses to ensure guests don't get lost. It is also a good idea to arrange for them to taxi people back to their accommodation or cars at the end of the night. The second concern is the size of the venue. Is it going to be big enough for all of your guests, particularly if you are inviting some people to the reception only? If you've fallen in love with a venue, but it's not large enough, it is worth enquiring whether they would allow a marquee to cater for extra numbers.

It is important to find a venue that matches the style of your day, so check out the interior decor as well as the outside of the building. If you want guests to stay over, then look for a venue with accommodation. It's not uncommon for party-mad brides and grooms to stay over too and hold a wedding breakfast in the morning. After all, if you've put that much effort in, you won't want to leave the fun.

Check to see whether the venue has on-site caterers or whether you will have to hire them, and find out if there are adequate parking facilities. You will be expected to pay a deposit when you book, which you usually forfeit if you have a change of mind, so visit as many venues as possible and make sure that you are 100 per cent happy before you give the go-head.

> ☺ It is often cheaper to hire wedding venues in the week rather than at weekends – but remember to check that your nearest and dearest will be able to attend.

Marquees

Marquees are ideal if you're having a summer wedding or if you've found your perfect venue but need some more space to hold all of your guests. They are a popular choice for weddings and parties because they are so flexible: you can erect one anywhere from your mum and dad's back lawn to a hillside. A good hire company will have a variety of different shaped marquees so you will be able to find one to suit your location and the size of your wedding party. Many brides like the fact that the interior is a blank canvas that can be decorated to their unique style. You'll have a choice of flooring, and linings, such as billowing white drapes or a cloth dotted with stars for that dining-under-the-night-sky feel.

Most marquee companies get booked up long before the summer wedding season, so you should start looking around seven to eight months before the wedding day. The company you choose should have experience of supplying marquees for weddings, and find out if the firm can help out with any other aspects of the reception, such as table and chair hire. Discuss with them the exact details of your wedding, and make sure that there's going to be enough room for a dining area and a dance area if you're having entertainment. Check that there's a heating system and air-conditioning system to ensure that your guests don't overheat or shiver during the reception.

Hotels/country houses
The joy of having your reception in a hotel is that everything you need is already there including, in most cases, the catering. Depending on your budget and the size of the hotel, you may want to hire a function room for the day and evening, or hire the whole hotel for 24 hours and invite close family and friends to spend the night there. This is an increasingly popular option, as it means that guests can have a drink at the reception.

At home

If you want to cut back on the amount of cash being spent, you could opt to have a reception at your house, or one your parents' houses. This will largely depend on space and access and how close the house is to the ceremony venue.

You will have to be prepared for the wedding to take over your home for weeks before the day itself and you should also be aware that there is potential for your home to be damaged if you have lots of guests turning up.

On the plus side, you will have total control over how you want to decorate your home – you can do anything you like with no grumpy hotel manager looking over your shoulder. You could also have a go at the catering yourself – ask close family and friends to help you to prepare the food beforehand. And, of course, there's no corkage to pay.

Things to consider include bathroom facilities – if it's a big wedding you may have to hire portaloos – and noise. You don't want your neighbours to be calling the police because you're creating a racket in the early hours of the morning. The best thing to do is to invite them all along!

Contingency plans

If you want to get married in the UK you are going to have to accept the fact that there is no guarantee of sunshine, so you'd be unwise to plan your whole wedding around an outside venue. If you do have your heart set on a drinks reception outside on the lawn, go for it, but have a Plan B just in case. Book a room so that guests can easily move inside in case of showers. A room with French windows that open out on to a terrace or lawn is ideal. On the other hand, if it turns out to be a sizzling hot day, check that there are umbrellas available for your guests to sit under for shade.

Looking after the guests

Your wedding day is about tying the knot, but it's also about celebrating your marriage with your friends and family, and you want them to enjoy it as much as possible. There are lots of ways to ensure this.

If you're having your reception in a different location to the ceremony, send your guests a map showing them how to get from one to the other. Some of your guests from out of town are going to be arriving the night before the wedding, so it's a good idea to find out where they will be staying and arrange for a welcome note and little goodie bag to be in their room on arrival. It won't cost much but it will be the perfect start to the wedding for them. It's also a great idea to ask hotel staff to place a chocolate by guests' beds with a thank-you note for coming to the wedding. Again the cost is minimal but the thought priceless.

If you're worried that you're not going to get to see enough of your guests on the wedding day, you could arrange a pre-wedding get-together for old friends. You may be incredibly busy in the run-up to the big day, but you can spare an hour or two to attend a dinner or drinks party. It will also help you to unwind.

Alternatively, more and more couples are having post-wedding breakfasts or lunches. This is a nice way to get together with close family and friends to chat about the day before and catch up with people that you didn't have time to see during the reception. It also means that tired guests don't have to rush straight home.

Should I have a guest book?

A guest book is a wonderful way of recording your wedding day. Buy a large, blank album, place it by the entrance to the reception and make a notice asking guests to write messages to the bride and groom in it. It's a good idea to place a pot of pens by it too as they tend to get lost quickly.

There are other ways to record guests' thoughts and memories too. Place a blank piece of card and little envelope at each place setting and put a dish on each table for people to drop their notes into – you'll have great fun reading them all when you get back from the honeymoon. Ask a friend to walk round with a hand-held camcorder for half an hour to interview guests, or to take Polaroid photos of everyone as they arrive at the ceremony. Then spread the pictures out on a table at the reception and ask guests to write a message on the back of their photograph.

Equipment hire

Reception venues usually supply the main items like tables, chairs and china. Check with them to see exactly what they do and don't supply and make a list of what, if anything, you need to hire. If they don't supply the bigger items, ask your catering company or marquee company, if applicable, about what they are able to supply. If none of the firms with which you're dealing are able to supply sufficient chairs, tables, china or glassware, you will have to approach a hire company. Only do this once you've a good idea about the exact numbers of people attending the wedding.

A checklist for the basics
- Candlesticks
- Chairs
- China

- Cutlery
- Glasses – red and white wine, champagne flutes and tumblers
- Jugs
- Napkins
- Salt and pepper pots
- Serving dishes, if necessary
- Tables
- Tablecloths
- Vases.

Before hiring any equipment you should enquire about transport costs to and from the venue, how long you can keep the items, charges for breakages and payment conditions. Also check to see whether you are expected to clean the items before they are returned and whether you need insurance.

Food

A large portion of your wedding budget will be spent on life's essentials: food and drink. A happy guest is one who is well fed and watered, so although it's okay to cut back in other areas, you shouldn't scrimp on the drink or nosh.

Traditionally a wedding breakfast is a seated, three- or four-course affair, but modern brides are increasingly opting for less formal receptions. A hot and cold buffet is an ideal way to ensure that there is something to suit everyone's palate and to let guests mix informally and arrange their own seating plans. Another chic alternative is to have food stalls dotted around your venue at which guests can help themselves to delicious nibbles that chefs prepare in front of them. Alternatively, you may want to provide canapés or a high tea for an afternoon reception. Some contemporary brides are even issuing reception invites to enjoy bangers and mash in a local pub, a barbecue or even a picnic on the beach.

If your venue doesn't have catering staff or facilities, you're going to have to hire an outside company. However, most venues that don't provide food themselves have contacts for professional caterers in the area. As always when hiring someone for your special day, check that they have lots of experience of catering for large numbers, preferably at weddings. Ask to try some food prepared by the company and also ask to see sample menus, which can provide inspiration for your own wedding too.

What food should we choose for our reception?

When it comes to choosing your menu, it's wise to base it around the season in which you're getting married. A summer wedding should focus on light ingredients such as fish and chicken, while winter wedding fare should be more hearty and comforting such as beef and lamb. Don't forget vegetarians, who will need a tasty alternative to meat-based dishes, such as mushroom risotto or stuffed peppers. Also discuss with your caterers an option for kids that is based on the theme of the main menu.

If you're opting for canapés, then make sure that there will be something to suit everyone's taste, young and old. Popular trends at the moment include mini fish-and-chip cones, complete with a handy little fork, or mini tortilla wraps. It is important that canapés are substantial and that you provide enough so that guests don't leave the reception hungry – allow for around eight to ten for each person.

If you're on a budget and are forking out a lot of money for a sit-down wedding breakfast, consider reducing your catering bill by buying your own snacks for the evening reception. Guests aren't going to need too much as they will have eaten a lot for lunch, so you could always ask close family members to arrange a DIY spread. Bowls of crisps, peanuts and cashew nuts are ideal to pick at, as are sushi, mini quiches and sandwiches, all of which can be bought from a supermarket in bulk.

☺ Save money by serving a vegetarian starter; that way you won't have to serve different dishes for veggies.

Drink

There are lots of choices here, so select a range that suits both the style of the wedding and your budget. Be realistic – is expensive vintage champagne really going to be appreciated at a party?

Champagne

Champagne is the drink of celebration, so it is perfect for wedding receptions. Whatever style of wedding you have, modern or traditional, champagne is a classic tipple that is ideal for toasts. However, the bubbly drink is expensive, so brides on a budget may want to consider a good quality sparkling wine, such as Cava, instead.

Shop around when choosing your champagne, trying supermarkets, off-licences and wine merchants, as there can be a big discrepancy in prices from one place to the next. The cost of individual bottles can vary enormously, from brands such as Albert Etienne which start at around £14 a bottle through to more expensive brands like Moët & Chandon and Cristal, so do your research, as you may discover a superior taste for a fraction of the price of the more famous brands. Ask to try samples and don't be afraid to ask for a discount if you're buying in bulk.

It is customary to serve up champagne or sparkling wine when guests first arrive at the reception venue, and then again for the speeches. Allow for two to three glasses of champagne per person, and you can squeeze around six glasses of champagne from a standard 75 cl bottle. It may be worth looking at magnums, which hold twice the amount as a normal bottle, as they can be favourably priced. For a hip option, you could offer guests mini bottles of champagne to sip through a straw, but, be warned, this can be incredibly expensive.

Wine

Wine is the ideal choice of alcohol to serve with your food. As a general rule allow half a bottle per person (around three glasses). However, only you know your wedding guests, so if you think they're going to need more then order in extra. The last thing you want is for your party to run dry.

Your choice of menu will dictate to some extent your choice of wine, but as a rule it's a good idea to get a selection of red and white wine. Don't think that you can only have white wine with chicken and fish and red with red meat. There are some light, fruity reds, which will go with anything, and rosé is also an option. However, rich, dense wines like Shiraz or Grenache should only be served with darker meat, while light, crisp wines, such as Chardonnay-based wines and Beaujolais are perfect accompaniments to chicken and fish.

If you're having a winter wedding, serving mulled wine at the start of the reception is an excellent way of warming guests up when they come in from the cold.

As with champagne, it is not necessarily true that the more you pay, the better the wine. Experts will tell you that there are some very acceptable table wines for under £10 per bottle from the major supermarkets. Your caterers should be able to give you sound advice on wine to complement your chosen menu, and most major supermarkets and off-licences will be able to put you in touch with one of their wine buyers if you need further assistance. Alternatively, if you are buying your own, it may be worth buying a wine guide which will list good makes and where they can be bought, and inform you about which foods they complement.

If you want to give your wine a personal touch, you could always arrange to have personalised labels put on the bottles, with your names and the date of the wedding. The Occasions Drinks Service at Wine Rack and Bottoms Up stores offers this service.

> ☺ Many wine retailers offer to hire out glasses free of charge if you place a large order with them.

Cocktails

The most chic drink of the new millennium is the cocktail, and there's no reason why you can't include it in your wedding day. Not only do cocktails taste divine, you can also have lots of fun choosing mixes that will match the colour scheme of your wedding. How about a deep red cosmopolitan or a curacao-based cocktail for something blue?

Cocktails are a cool alternative to offer guests when they arrive, particularly if they are champagne-based. Popular choices include bucks fizz (a mix of champagne and orange juice), bellini (champagne with peach juice) and kir royale which has a splash of cassis. For a summer wedding, incorporate fruit into the recipes. You could serve sea breeze (a mix of cranberry and vodka) or use strawberries as a garnish – they look particularly pretty on the rim of a glass.

Non-alcoholic cocktails are also a wonderfully tasty option for any guests who are tee-total or driving and also for children who are bound to love the funky colours.

What is corkage?
It is usual for venues with their own catering service to want to use champagne and wine from their own suppliers. This can be very expensive, but on the plus side it means that you will receive expert advice about the best wines to choose for your reception and will also only be charged for bottles that you drink.

If you do want to bring your own alcohol to the reception, and the venue doesn't mind, you must be prepared to pay corkage on each bottle. This is a charge that hotels make for opening a bottle that you have supplied on their premises as compensation for profit lost as a result of not supplying the alcohol themselves. It also takes into account the cost of the waiters having to chill, open and serve the wine. Do your calculations carefully, as some venues can charge up to £20 to open expensive champagne.

How do we devise the table plans?
If you're having a sit-down reception meal, there is usually a top table for members of the wedding party. Traditionally this is a long table facing the rest of the guests, ensuring that everyone gets a good view of the happy couple. The bride and groom sit in the middle, with the

groom on the bride's right, and whoever is making the first speech, usually the father of the bride, on her left. If parents are divorced they should be seated close to their new partners.

If you don't want a formal top table, there are plenty of other options. Why not sit at a round table so that you're facing each other rather than the rest of the guests. Or the bride and groom could sit at their own table, like Victoria and David Beckham at their reception. If you've got some serious family politics, why not involve your parents in compiling the seating plan, which will make them feel wanted and hopefully avoid any family upsets.

A seating plan for the rest of the wedding guests isn't vital, but it does help to make things run more smoothly. A table plan at the entrance to the dining room will enable guests to go directly to their seats, where you should also have placed name cards.

Traditional top-table seating plan

Chief bridesmaid	Groom's father	Bride's mother	Groom	Bride	Bride's father	Groom's mother	Best man

Bride's parents are divorced and both have remarried

Bride's stepfather	Chief bridesmaid	Groom's father	Bride's mother	Groom	Bride	Bride's father	Groom's mother	Best man	Bride's stepmother

Groom's parents are divorced and both parents have remarried

Best man	Groom's stepmother	Groom's father	Bride's mother	Groom	Bride	Bride's father	Groom's mother	Groom's stepfather	Chief bridesmaid

Both sets of parents have divorced and remarried

Groom's stepmother	Bride's stepfather	Chief bridesmaid	Groom's father	Bride's mother	Groom	Bride	Bride's father	Groom's mother	Best man	Bride's stepmother	Groom's stepfather

What about the rest of the wedding guests?

Bridesmaids, ushers and close relatives are usually seated close to the top table. It's a good idea to place couples at the same table but not necessarily next to each other. Men and women are usually alternated. If you know there are guests coming to the wedding who don't get on, it's wise to separate them, but don't worry too much about it – this is your big day and they will have to put aside their differences.

The ideal seating arrangement is for everyone to be near someone they know but also to have the opportunity to meet new people. If you've both got lots of eligible single friends, why not try a bit of matchmaking and have a singles' table? If you've got a few teenagers coming to the wedding, they may prefer a separate table. Small children can be seated with their parents, but if they're under the age of six or seven, it may be preferable to hire a childminder or arrange a crèche. If there are going to be several tots in tow, you could hire a room in the venue and organise some entertainment to keep them amused and out of trouble.

If you don't want to go down the formal route and would prefer something more casual, you could let guests simply mingle. This works well with a buffet-style reception. Arrange tables and chairs around the edge of the room and let guests sort out their own table companions. If you're serving up canapés, it is still worth making sure there are plenty of chairs available for those who don't want to stand, particularly elderly relatives.

Can I make a speech?

Yes! It's as simple as that. Although the bride doesn't traditionally make a speech, times have changed since they made the 'rules' so there is nothing to stop you saying a few words on your wedding day.

Traditionally the bride's father (or his equivalent) kicks off the proceedings after the food has been served and before the cutting of the cake. His speech generally welcomes guests, toasts the groom's parents, and offers some advice to the newly-weds. It is also usual to welcome the new son-in-law to the family and to finish by toasting the happiness of the bride and groom.

The next speech is performed by the groom who thanks various wedding guests, particularly those who have helped out, and pays tribute to his new bride. He finishes by thanking both sets of parents and giving a toast to the bridesmaids.

The final speech, and arguably the hardest because guests expect it to be funny, is the best man's. As well as telling some amusing anecdotes, he must also remember to thank the groom on behalf of the bridesmaids, read out any telegrams from absent friends and toast the bride and groom and host and hostess.

It may seem that this running order leaves little space for you, but an ideal time to say a few words is before or after the groom's speech. Make sure that you know exactly what you're going to say – don't be tempted simply to stand up and 'say a few words' as you're sure to end up tongue-tied. Write a speech and practise it, and slip small cue cards into your bag on the day to prompt you.

> ☺ If you want to do something a little more unusual, what about writing a poem dedicated to your new hubby or even singing a love song?

Decorating the tables

Deciding the finer details of your wedding can be just as much fun as choosing the big items like the dress and flowers, so give some thought to decorating your reception tables.

Favours

It has become usual to give little gifts to your guests as a token of thanks for coming and as a reminder of your special day. Traditionally, five sugared almonds representing health, wealth, happiness, longevity and fertility are given in a box to each guest, but modern brides now offer all kinds of treats. Popular ideas include chocolates, candles, packets of flower seeds or miniature pots of flowers. It is also a great idea to use your favours as name places, which will save time and money. For example, have cookies iced with guests' names or boxes of sweets with name tags attached.

Although relatively small, the cost of favours does mount up, particularly if you are having a large wedding, so if you are on a tight budget you need to think about whether they are necessary at all, or perhaps you may prefer to make your own. This is simpler than it sounds, and is a way of adding a personal touch. Ideas include filling little boxes with sugared almonds, jelly beans or Smarties, and tying them with ribbon. Or how about baking your own cookies? Buy a heart-shaped cutter for an ultra-romantic sweet treat. Surprise your guests with cracker favours, which you fill with a tiny gift. This is perfect for a Christmas reception, or for any other time of year, and gets your guests interacting straight away. Other fun favours include bubbles, sparklers and party poppers.

Napkins
Use your napkins as another way to bring decoration to the table. Wrap them in ribbon, tuck flowers into folded ones or fan them out. Hire or buy coloured napkins that will stand out on a white plate. If you've got money to burn, you could have them embroidered with the initials of the bride and groom and the date of the wedding. Marabou feathers are perfect for livening up a dull napkin.

Centrepieces
The obvious choice for centrepieces is flowers, but there are lots of other ideas that will impress your guests. A centrepiece made of fruit is a chic and tasty alternative, as guests pick at the display during the

meal. The fruit you decide to use will depend on the season, but strawberries, raspberries and grapes look good in the summer. Bowls full of one type of fruit inject vibrant colour into the proceedings. The bright acid colours of lemons and oranges work particularly well and are also far cheaper than flowers. Candles are an extremely popular centrepiece with modern girls-in-the-know, who appreciate that not only do they look great, but the light they give off is incredibly flattering. You could opt for candle holders, or use floating candles and rose petals in a bowl of water on each table for a harmonious feel.

The cake

One of the most memorable parts of the day will be when you cut your cake. It's a great photo opportunity and symbolic of your new unity, but more importantly it will be a taste sensation if you've chosen well!

Choosing a cake designer

You may have a clear idea about the sort of cake you want for your reception, or you may not have a clue. Either way, as soon as you've booked the venue, you should start sourcing cake designers. It's important that you order the cake well in advance as most good cake designers will need at least a couple of months' notice to prepare your dream cake, sometimes even longer in the height of the summer wedding season. Use friends' recommendations, Yellow Pages and wedding fayres to track down reputable cake makers in your area, and make appointments to see at least two so that you can compare service and prices.

As with all wedding services, it's important that you see evidence of the cake maker's expertise, so ask to see photographs of cakes they've made for weddings, not just brochure shots, and also have a look at cakes they may have in their shop or studio. Once you've decided on your designer, it's time for the fun part. Arrange for a tasting session, at which you get to try out lots of gorgeous cake and pick which one you like best. It may sound like a day in heaven, but it's also very important as you want a cake that tastes as good as it looks.

Once you've chosen your cake mix, delay ordering it until you've drawn up the final guest list. You don't want to end up with one tier of iced fruit cake to feed 200 hungry friends and relatives. When you have got your final number, it's always a good idea to add a few on, because you may have unexpected guests or want to send pieces to people who couldn't make it.

What style of cake should I choose?
American-style stacked tiers are currently in vogue. Dressed up with flowers or pretty ribbon, they are ideal for a contemporary reception. Tiers of cake mounted on columns are also making a comeback. Tiny cup cakes are also big news in cake design, either piled up in tiers to form a cake shape, or placed individually on each guest's plate. Other fun styles include the dramatic croquembouche, a pyramid of cream-filled pastry buns, and ice-cream, which is best as a pudding. Novelty wedding cakes are another big trend, with everything from footballs to pianos cropping up in modern cake designs. Not only does it give you the chance to personalise your cake, it's also bound to raise some smiles.

What's the best filling for a wedding cake?
Fruit cake covered with marzipan and icing has long been the favoured choice for wedding cakes. If you want to preserve some of the cake –

maybe for the christening of your first child – or want to send a slice off to relatives who couldn't make it to the wedding, then it remains the best option.

For brides who shiver at the thought of fruit cake, there are lots of other tasty alternatives. If you're the sort of girl who can never have enough chocolate, then you'll love the fact that chocolate cakes, of every variety, are now the wedding-day favourite. You're guaranteed to get very little waste if you plump for this – guests will be scraping up every last crumb. Do bear in mind, however, that chocolate might not be a suitable if your wedding is in the summer. Carrot cake or lemon sponge, with a jam or lemon filling, are both sure to be popular with guests. The key is to go for something that most people enjoy, not just your own personal favourite. If you want to provide a choice, why not ask for three tiers of cake, each with a different filling?

How should the cake be decorated?

The decoration of the cake is usually inspired by the theme of the wedding. If you're getting married by the sea, for example, you could decorate it with shells and pearls, or if your colour scheme is lilac and silver then lilac flowers and a silver sash around the cake is ideal. If you want fresh flowers or fruit to decorate your cake, chat to your florist about designs and colour schemes. Some couples want their cake to reflect their personalities and hobbies, and choose sugarcraft models such as a groom playing cricket or a bride playing tennis to liven up a traditional cake. Figurines are not as popular as they used to be, but you can now buy some fabulous designs, such as the bride holding the groom in her arms, that are guaranteed to amuse your guests.

How can I save money on the cake?

Lots of factors influence the price of the wedding cake. Caterers usually come up with a sum based on how much your cake will be per slice, and then calculate a figure according to how many guests you have. The slice price can vary from a couple of pounds to over £10, depending on what sort of cake you choose. As a rule, the simpler the cake, the cheaper it is. Anything handmade and labour intensive, such as sugar flowers or chocolate roses, is going to cost a lot more than a plain iced cake. Some supermarkets sell very good quality cakes: Marks & Spencer has introduced a line of wedding cakes with tiers of various sizes which you can mix and match.

If you're a decent cook it's easy to bake the cake yourself. The icing can be more difficult, however, so you could always take a basic cake to a professional and ask for it to be covered and decorated. If you want to have a go yourself, most supermarkets sell fondant icing which you can roll out and smooth over the outside of the cake. For decoration, stick to ribbons and flowers unless you are a dab hand at sugarcraft or have a friend who you could ask to help out – he or she is likely to be extremely flattered.

Music

Music is a style-setter, so even if music is in the background, it can have quite an impact on the atmosphere you are trying to establish. That means it is worth some serious thought.

Post-ceremony

While the photographs are being taken and your guests are sipping champagne, you might want to lay on some music. If your ceremony and reception are in separate venues, travel between the two will take up some of the time, so you won't have as long to keep guests entertained before the meal and speeches. However, if ceremony and reception are taking place in the same venue, you may need to arrange some entertainment immediately after guests leave the ceremony.

At this point it's best to keep it up-beat and lively, but not a main focus of attention, as guests will want to chat. If the budget permits, the perfect solution is a string quartet, which serves as great background music for both small and large gatherings. If you're having a summer wedding, you can arrange for the quartet to play outside.

> ☺ A more unusual option is a harpist. The soothing sounds make enchanting background music and it looks fantastic.

First dance

Depending on whether you're a disco diva or a delicate wallflower, your first dance is either heaven or hell. If you are not looking forward to the idea of all eyes being on you while you strut your stuff, get over your nerves by thinking of all those clubs where you've danced without a care in the world. Also, when it's time for your first dance, you will already have been through the most nerve-wracking bit of the day, the ceremony, and this is a chance to let your hair down and dance with your man – so enjoy it.

If you're both nervous about this, why not invest in a couple of dance lessons so you'll feel really confident when you take centre stage? Lots of couples have a dilemma about which song to choose for the first dance: too slow and it's difficult to move, too fast and you'll end up wiggling your hips in an unromantic fashion and tripping over your dress.

Traditionally, the bride and groom danced to a waltz, but if ballroom dancing has never been your thing and you prefer *Dirty Dancing* to *Come Dancing* then look for something a little more modern.

Favourite first dance tunes include:
- 'Unforgettable', Natalie and Nat King Cole
- 'Wonderful Tonight', Eric Clapton
- 'From This Moment On', Shania Twain
- 'When a Man Loves a Woman', Percy Sledge/Michael Bolton
- 'Everything I Do, (I Do it for You)', Bryan Adams
- 'What a Wonderful World', Louis Armstrong
- 'When You Say Nothing At All', Ronan Keating

Disco

Think of a wedding reception, and you think of a disco. There's no doubt that a disco does get everyone up and dancing, providing the music is right. It's also a cheaper alternative to hiring live musicians. If you want to hire a disco and DJ check with your venue that there is room for a dance floor, that high noise levels won't be a problem and also what time music can be played until.

If you get the go-ahead, it's worth asking the venue if they have any contacts for disco hire. If not, the best places to start looking are the Yellow Pages, classified ads in music and wedding magazines and the internet. Ask friends for recommendations or, if you have a friend who is into music, ask them to help out.

If possible, try to see the DJ in action on a night out. Discuss play lists, and make sure that he or she has the sort of tunes that you'll be happy to dance to, and a good mix of old and new music to satisfy all tastes and ages. Find out whether lighting has to be hired separately and also establish how long you want him or her to play for, including breaks. Check for any hidden costs, like travelling expenses, and find out if the equipment is insured for damage.

Live music

If you're tempted to hire a live act there are some important points to consider. Always go and listen to the band before you hire to see whether they really can perform well live and to see what sort of atmosphere they create. Don't rely on CDs or tapes, which may have been enhanced in a studio. Find out if the band will tailor their style and play list to fit your preferences. If they only play their own material, you'll want to know that it is the sort of music that will get people up and dancing.

Consider the size of the venue before you book the band. Is it going to be big enough to hold a band, their equipment and all your guests? Will the acoustics be good enough? Is there space for them to unload and load all of their equipment easily?

Bands usually start from £500 upwards for a night's hire, and remember that they are going to need some food and drink during the night, so add this on to your catering budget.

Cover-version bands are always a hit, particularly well-known groups like Abba or The Beatles, and some brides and grooms have even been know to hire an Elvis impersonator for the night.

If a pop or rock band isn't your cup of tea, but you do want some live entertainment, why not look at alternatives like a steel band or a jazz quartet. People love something a little bit adventurous, and it crosses age barriers.

It might sound old-fashioned but a barn dance is a fantastic way of getting everyone up and dancing, young and old. Hire a compère who can talk everyone through the routines and you're guaranteed to have all your guests up, linking arms, particularly after the drink has been flowing.

For more exotic fun, which will get pulses racing, you could hire a salsa band for later in the evening. Learning new dance moves is always fun, and routines involve different dance partners so it means your guests will get to know each other.

Entertainment

If a disco or live band isn't your thing, then there are lots of other fantastic ways to wow your guests. How about turning the venue into a casino? Ask guests to dress up in black tie just like James Bond, bring in roulette wheels and encourage people to gamble the night away with fake money handed out at the door.

Make the celebration go with a bang by forking out for a huge outside firework display. It will make your bill soar, but the ooohhs and ahhhhs will be more than worth it.

If money isn't an issue, you could hire some fairground rides for guests to whiz around on. A less expensive option is a bouncy castle, which can be hired for around £200.

How do we keep children amused at the reception?

A wedding is a long day for children, and children – especially young ones – have a short attention span. You want to keep them amused but also involved. If you've got lots of kids coming, it may be worth investing in a professional carer to watch over them, and if you've got babies and tots on the invites, then a mobile crèche company could be the answer.

If the children are a bit older or you want to reduce the costs, then you can think about other ways of keeping them amused. Target the times when their interest is likely to flag, such as at the reception drinks and during the speeches, and make plans. Proven successes include treasure hunts – ask an usher to plant some sweets around the grounds of the venue before the wedding. Compile a wedding-day quiz, with lots of questions for them to find the answers to, such as the name of the bride's mother or how many bridesmaids there are. Let them know that there is a good prize for the winner, but also provide smaller gifts, such as chocolates, for all the children who take part.

If you want them to play a direct part in the wedding, you could give them fun jobs to do, which will keep them amused and also make them feel part of the day. The obvious choice is to make them flower girls or pageboys. Alternatively, they could be asked to hand out flowers to the wedding party, help to serve canapés, take snaps with disposable cameras or ask guests to sign the visitors' book.

The send-off

Even hip, modern brides might still want a traditional send-off from their friends, so make sure there are things on hand for guests to use to ensure you have a spectacular departure. Paper confetti is still popular, but it's not favoured by some venues, as it is hard to clean up. Buy a biodegradable type and place boxes of it around the venue exit, or ask ushers to hand it out before you're about to leave. A great alternative to confetti is rose petals: not only do they look elegant they also smell great. Bubbles are now very popular at weddings. Place a little bubble pot in each place setting and attach a tag with a note asking your guests to use it at the end of the night. The Swiss traditionally throw wrapped sweets at newly-weds, but if the thought of being struck on the forehead by a boiled sweet doesn't appeal, how about a softer alternative like marshmallows?

> ☺ If you're going to be leaving after dark, you could supply sparklers to wave – the photographs will look spectacular.

Be prepared for the wedding car to be decorated by guests. This usually involves streamers, tin cans and a 'Just Married' sign being attached to the bumper. If you're not leaving in your own transport, be on your guard for other surprises, such as confetti in your suitcase.

Reception timetable

If you want your wedding day to run like clockwork, then you're going to have to be organised. Prepare a reception timetable so that you can ensure everything goes smoothly in exactly the order it's meant to. Below is an example to give you an idea of what is supposed to happen when – use it as a start for your own schedule. This is based on a formal wedding so yours may well be much more informal.

3pm: Meet and greet

Having a receiving line as your guests arrive at the reception venue is a great way to say hello to everyone and to thank them for coming. Usually the line consists of the main members of the wedding party in the following order: bride's mother, bride's father, bride, groom, chief bridesmaid, best man.

If you want something a little less imposing, the bride and groom could be the ones to meet and greet guests. Or you may want to circulate and mingle with your guests, chatting to them informally.

3–4pm: Drink up

It is usual to allocate an hour to an hour-and-a-half at the beginning to the reception to allow guests to sip their drinks and chat to friends, and for photographs to be taken. This is traditionally called the cocktail hour and is typically held outside, if possible, or in a room separate to the dining area. It allows the bride and groom to catch up with friends and relatives and also gives guests time to check seating plans and dining arrangements.

It is a good idea to arrange for some hors d'oeuvres to be brought in, as alcohol on an empty stomach is a recipe for disaster! Also, you may want to hire a band or play some music as the perfect background soundtrack.

4.15pm: Dinner is announced

Dinner is announced by the head waiter, DJ or band. The wedding party usually enter the dining room first and are seated before the rest of the guests come through. If the bride and groom want to make a dramatic entrance, they can wait until everyone is sitting down before coming into the dining room.

4.30pm: Invitation to eat

Once everyone, including the bride and groom, is seated, the bride's father, or the person who is allocated that role, welcomes everyone and invites them to eat. If there is a blessing, it can be said by a minister, if he or she has been invited to the wedding reception, or by a parent.

4.45pm: First course
The first course is served to the wedding party and then the complimentary wine is served. If you're having a buffet-style reception, the guests are invited to help themselves to the food.

5.10pm: Next course
The first course is cleared from the top tables and then the rest of the room, and the subsequent courses follow. It is important that enough time is given for guests to enjoy their food and wine, but that they don't have to wait too long between each course.

6.45pm: Speeches
When pudding has been cleared away, guests' champagne glasses will be filled in preparation for the toasts. The bride's father makes the first speech and toasts the health of the bride and groom. The groom then makes a speech responding to his father-in-law on behalf of himself and his wife. He also proposes a toast to the bridesmaids. The best man replies on behalf of the bridesmaids and then makes his speech.

7.30pm: Cake-cutting
The bride and groom cut the cake, which can then be served with coffee. If you want to serve your cake as pudding, the cutting can be scheduled earlier in the reception order.

8pm: First dance
The couple take to the floor for the first dance. The next track is reserved for the bride and her father, and the groom and his mother. When these dances are over, the rest of the guests can take to the floor.

Departing
If you're leaving the wedding party to stay somewhere else for the first night, you will change and then say goodbye to the guests, usually whilst being showered with confetti. This is also the ideal time for the bride to gather her single friends and throw her bouquet. Remember that whoever catches it is destined to tie the knot next – so aim well!

If you're the sort of couple who can't bear to leave a good party, you may delay your departure until the last guest leaves.

The wedding car
The groom usually picks the transport for the wedding day, but you may want to give him a few gentle hints so that he doesn't simply go for the fastest, shiniest car in the garage.

1   If you're wearing a large, full-skirted gown then it's got to be large enough to fit you, your groom and your dress inside easily.
2   If you pick a white car and you're wearing a white dress, you won't stand out on any wedding photographs taken next to it – so think about opting for a car with colour instead.
3   Think about the time of year that you're getting married. Soft-top cars always seem very romantic, but you won't think that when you arrive with your expensive new hairstyle blown into a frizzy mess. And if it's autumn or winter, it'll also be extremely cold.

4   Some car hire companies will decorate the car, but you may want to discuss this with your florist, and you must be prepared for your wedding guests to sabotage the transport with ribbons, streamers and confetti.

5   There are alternatives to a car. A horse and carriage is a traditional option, or if your reception is by a river you could romantically row off into the sunset. Or why not leave in hot-air balloon? Well, budget for a start, but it's surely the most glamorous exit!

Chapter 9
Gifts

You don't have to have a gift list for your wedding. Some couples simply leave it up to their guests to choose the wedding presents. However, a gift list does avoid the ten toasters problem and saves any present-duplication embarrassment for your guests. Guests often appreciate a helping hand as it gives them ideas and guidance about what you really want and need. After all, no one likes buying a present that isn't wanted.

Choosing your gift list

Any shopaholic worth her salt will be drooling in anticipation of a gift list. It's an opportunity to get lots of fabulous items that you wouldn't usually have been able to buy.

Gift lists were first introduced as a way of making sure that couples living together for the first time had all of the basics that they would need to set up home. If you're moving in together after the wedding or are buying a new flat or house after the big day, then it's an ideal opportunity to ask for items for your home. For basic household items like kettles, toasters and fridges, you're best to start looking on the high street. Stores such as John Lewis, Debenhams and House of Fraser all have dedicated wedding departments to help you compile your list. If you can't decide exactly what you need, you can always ask guests to purchase vouchers from the store for you to spend at a later date.

If you've been living together for a while and have all of the basic items you need, you could use your gift list either to up-date them or to ask for presents which are more of a luxury, such as sets of crystal glasses, fine china and designer cutlery. For this kind of item you would be better approaching a gift-list company, which will have a team of experts who will be able to advise you on a huge number of specialist items for you home.

If you've no need or desire to ask for presents for your home, there are other options. Some couples ask for cash, but usually just from parents and very close relatives who may want to contribute towards a large item such as a flat deposit or honeymoon. There are other ways to ensure that you get to spend money on what you want. You could ask guests to buy honeymoon vouchers instead of gifts. Companies such as Thomas Cook Wedding List Service, British Airways Travel Shops and Abercrombie & Kent all offer this service.

If you want unusual gifts, then there are now specialist companies set up, like Bliss and Confetti, which offer lots of exciting trips, from hot-air ballooning to spa treatments. If you're one of the lucky few who has everything you could possibly need, you could always take your cue from film stars Catherine Zeta Jones and Michael Douglas who asked guests to donate money to a charity fund set up for their baby son Dylan.

How it works

Most department stores and specialist shops will have a gift-list service which will help you to choose exactly what you want and compile a comprehensive list. Remember that there's nothing to stop you having a gift list at more than one store.

You will be invited to walk around the store with a form or electronic pen selecting items for your list, which will then be transferred to computer. Walking round a large department store can be exhausting, so you may want to do this in a couple of trips in order to give it your full concentration – and wear comfy shoes! If it isn't possible to select your gifts in person, there will usually be a catalogue or web site.

What do we ask for?

Bear in mind who is coming to your wedding when selecting the gifts. It's important that you get things that you need and want, but there should be a good range of prices on the list so that people can pay out as little or as much as they want and don't feel forced to spend more than they had intended.

Once the list has been put on to a computer, guests will be able to phone up or buy a gift in person, and the records will be regularly updated, detailing who has bought what. It is worth finding a gift-list company that can also put your wedding list on the internet. Guests can then see the presents before they purchase, which is particularly useful for people who live abroad or who can't easily get to your chosen store.

Some companies offer a gift-wrapping service, often incurring an extra charge, and will also deliver. Guests may want to buy and wrap their own presents and bring them to the wedding, so arrange with the best man to have these delivered to your house while you're on your first night or honeymoon.

☺ Make sure your insurance covers you for theft while you're away.

Wedding present checklist

If you're going to ask for household products, it's a good idea to spend some time together making a list of exactly what you think you need. Make a list at home, wandering from room to room, noting down items you want or want to replace. You can then use this as a blueprint for the final list. Use the directory below as a starting point.

Kitchen electrical items
❑ Blender
❑ Bread maker
❑ Cooker
❑ Deep-fat fryer
❑ Espresso maker
❑ Freezer
❑ Fridge
❑ Ice-cream maker
❑ Kettle
❑ Pressure cooker
❑ Sandwich maker
❑ Toaster

❑ Juicer
❑ Kitchen knives
❑ Pestle and mortar
❑ Roasting tray
❑ Rolling pin
❑ Salt and pepper mills
❑ Saucepans
❑ Scales
❑ Spice rack
❑ Steamer
❑ Trivet
❑ Wine rack
❑ Wok

Useful kitchen items
❑ Aprons
❑ Baking tins
❑ Baking trays
❑ Bread board
❑ Cafetière
❑ Corkscrew
❑ Garlic press

Cutlery
❑ Knives (small and large)
❑ Forks (small and large)
❑ Dessert spoons
❑ Soup spoons
❑ Teaspoons
❑ Butter knives
❑ Steak knives

- Fish knives
- Fish slice
- Ladle
- Serving spoons

Crockery
- Dinner plates
- Side plates
- Soup bowls
- Soup tureen
- Salad bowl
- Egg cups
- Fruit bowl
- Teapot
- Cups and saucers
- Mugs
- Coffee cups and saucers
- Sugar bowl
- Milk jug
- Vegetable dishes

Glassware
- White wine glasses
- Red wine glasses
- Champagne flutes
- Sherry glasses
- Shot glasses
- Brandy glasses
- Decanters

- Tumblers
- Glass bowl
- Jugs
- Vases

Linen
- Sheets
- Duvet covers
- Mattress covers
- Pillow cases
- Electric blanket
- Valence
- Towels
- Bathrobes
- Bath mat
- Face cloths
- Napkins
- Tablecloth

Bedroom
- Pillows
- Duvet
- Chest of drawers
- Bedside cabinet
- Bed
- Chair
- Rug
- Mirror
- Lamp

Bathroom
- ☐ Cabinet
- ☐ Scales
- ☐ Shower curtain
- ☐ Soap holder
- ☐ Toiletries
- ☐ Toothbrush holder

Lounge
- ☐ Clock
- ☐ Cushions
- ☐ Lamp
- ☐ Ornaments
- ☐ Paintings
- ☐ Radio
- ☐ Rugs
- ☐ Sofa
- ☐ Speakers
- ☐ Stereo
- ☐ Television
- ☐ Throws

General
- ☐ Books
- ☐ Camcorder
- ☐ CDs
- ☐ Iron
- ☐ Ironing board
- ☐ Linen basket
- ☐ Luggage
- ☐ Photo frames
- ☐ Vacuum cleaner
- ☐ Videos
- ☐ Waste bins

Garden
- ☐ DIY tools
- ☐ Garden furniture
- ☐ Garden pots
- ☐ Gardening wear
- ☐ Patio heater
- ☐ Plants
- ☐ Stepladder

☺ Make sure your gift list covers a broad price range so that there is something in there to suit low and high budgets.

When you've compiled a list of what you think you need, it's time to match the list with the number of people coming to the wedding. Be realistic – it's no use having 100 items on there if you've only invited 30 people. It is a good idea to put a few more on the list than is needed, however, so that there is always a choice, even for people buying last minute when the majority of gifts have been snapped up.

Lots of stores give a discount on any remaining gifts, or vouchers to the value of a percentage of your guests' total spend, which you can put towards any outstanding gifts. Don' t make your list ridiculously long, however, or you'll end up with incomplete sets of everything, which means you'll either have to mix and match or have to fork out and buy the rest. Check the availability of each item with the store before it goes on the final list – you don't want to discover that your patterned plates have been discontinued after six months.

Who sent what?

You'll need to keep track of who sent what so that you can send out thank-you notes after the wedding. Some couples like to do this by hand, while others rely on information sent to them by their gift-list company detailing who has bought what.

If you do choose to keep your own record of presents as and when they come in, why not buy a special book to write it in? You could add your entries to a stylish book with blank pages or use a printed wedding journal. It allows you to see at a glance who has bought what and is also a great memento of the day. Combine it with your invitation and RSVP records to avoid writing out guests' names and addresses twice.

Should we buy gifts for the wedding party?

It's customary to buy a gift for each member of the wedding party to say thank you for playing such a big part in your special day. You don't have to spend a huge amount, however, as they are simply tokens of thanks and a memento of the day.

> ☺ The best time to give your gifts is the night before the wedding, possibly at a rehearsal dinner. Alternatively have them delivered to rooms on the morning of the wedding, if possible.

Maid of honour

She's been your right-hand woman, so you'll want to get her something extra special. Jewellery is always a popular choice, such as a silver bangle inscribed with your names.

Bridesmaids

It's best to get matching presents so that everyone is treated equally. Perfect presents include a bottle of perfume, chocolates, a silk purse, a charm bracelet, an engraved powder compact and lipstick – or how about silk, embroidered pyjamas for a luxury pressie?

Mothers

Your mum and mother-in-law will have undoubtedly got more than a little stressed in the run-up to the wedding, so the perfect gift is a voucher for a day at a health spa or individual treatments, such as massages, facials and manicures. Vouchers for a favourite department store are a good choice for shopaholics. You could plan a day for a shopping spree and take them to lunch too. A symbolic plant, such as a wedding rose, would be ideal for the mum with green fingers.

Best man
Best men have a reputation to maintain, so you'll want to buy your right-hand man a suitable gift. How about a leather Little Black Book and silver pen for all those girls' numbers he'll collect at the reception, or a tankard with his name and the date of the wedding inscribed and a bottle of champagne. Cuff links always seem to turn up on these lists, but ask yourself how often your best man would ever wear them.

Fathers
Best stick to traditional gifts like whisky and cigars for your dad and the other new man in your life. A hip flask engraved with the date of the wedding is a smart choice.

Ushers
Keep it simple by buying pens or tankards. A less conventional, but undoubtedly popular, choice would be a batch of tickets for a forthcoming sporting event like a football or rugby match.

Your groom
You'll want to buy him something extra special for your wedding day. What about a beautiful watch with a special message engraved on the back and a note in the box saying it should ensure he gets to the church on time? On the morning of the wedding, arrange for a buttonhole to be delivered to his door with a note declaring your everlasting love, and saying how much you are looking forward to the day ahead.

Chapter 10
The Honeymoon

Traditionally, it's the groom's job to pick and pay for the honeymoon, but unless you want a total surprise, it's common in modern marriages for both of you to choose where you want to go. Sun, sand and sea are the honeymoon norm, as this is the time to relax and chill out after the hectic wedding preparations and big day. Other ways of spending some quality time together as Mr and Mrs are on a cruise or a safari, on a visit to a city or country that neither of you have visited before, or maybe you want to enjoy a shared hobby together – such as diving, skiing or sailing.

Choosing your destination

To gain inspiration, pay a visit to a travel agent, who will be able to provide you with ideas and basic information about your options, and offer special honeymoon deals. Other good sources of information are the internet and travel and wedding magazines which usually have a section dedicated to honeymoons. Your choice of honeymoon destination will depend on how much time and money you have available, and how you want to spend this very special holiday.

This may be the ideal opportunity to take part in a pastime that you both enjoy – it may even have been the way that you met! Walking, cycling or climbing may sound like hard work to some of us, but to others it's the perfect way to recover from the wedding day. How about trekking in the Himalayas? Or maybe there's an activity that you've both always wanted to try out. Less energetic interests, such as painting or photography, could be the focus for your trip. Champagne tasting in France has a romantic ring to it – while whale watching in South Africa or husky-dog racing in Lapland sound more exotic.

If you have less than a week, you may want to go short haul so that you don't lose too much time getting to your destination. You could opt for a city honeymoon, with Venice, Paris, Barcelona, Rome and Florence all being romantic choices that will provide you with lots of opportunities for sightseeing and sharing candlelit meals. If it's the sun that you're after, but distance is an issue, then ideal hot spots include the Amalfi coast in Italy, Cyprus, Majorca, France and Portugal.

If you've got ten days or more for your honeymoon, then you can think about going long haul. Honeymoon favourites include the Caribbean, Indian Ocean, Australia and the United States. If you're a beach lover, Caribbean islands like Barbados and St Lucia are ideal, and the Indian Ocean islands of Mauritius, Seychelles and the Maldives are paradise. If you're the sort of couple who would get bored lying on a beach all day, ignore the obvious destinations and look at a honeymoon location with lots to see and do like Mexico, New Zealand or South Africa.

More and more couples are combining the two, and having a week relaxing on a beach before jetting off somewhere else for adventure and sightseeing. Dream two-destination honeymoons include a week in Mauritius followed by a safari in Africa; lying on a beach in Dubai then trekking in the Himalayas or flopping on a beach in Bermuda then hitting the shops in New York. Of course you may not want sun at all: some couples prefer snow and ice and head for ski resorts for an active honeymoon on the slopes.

If you do want sun, it's vital that you check out the weather in your dream destination. This list indicates the best times of year to visit.

- **Argentina:** September–May
- **Australia:** November–March
- **Brazil:** All year
- **Caribbean:** November–March
- **Chile:** September–April
- **Dubai:** All year
- **Ecuador and Galapagos:** All year
- **Greece:** May–October
- **Guyana:** All year
- **India:** October–March
- **Indonesia:** June–October
- **Italy:** May–October
- **Madagascar:** April–October
- **Malawi:** May–October
- **Malaysia:** June–September & November–March
- **Maldives:** December–April
- **Mauritius:** August–December
- **Mexico:** October–March
- **Morocco:** October–May
- **Peru:** All year
- **Seychelles:** June–October
- **South Africa:** October–April
- **Spain:** March–October
- **Tanzania and Uganda:** July–February
- **Thailand:** June–March
- **Vietnam:** November–February

Budget tips

Your honeymoon is probably the most expensive holiday you'll have in your life, but there's no rule that says it has to cost the earth. There are lots of ways to cut down costs but still ensure you have the trip of a lifetime. Wherever you go, tell people that you're honeymooners. Don't be shy, because you'll be amazed at how many free upgrades, complimentary bottles of champagne, fruit baskets, gifts and extra service you'll get if you let people know. Don't just limit yourself to hotels; travel agents and airlines love those in love too, and you're likely to get some great packages because of it.

A sure way to avoid huge costs is to pick a destination that's out of season. This doesn't mean you have to travel to Mauritius in the rainy season, but look to book at the beginning or end of peak season for lower costs. Also avoid holiday periods like July and August, or May Bank Holiday which tend to be the times when prices rise.

For your first-night accommodation, be aware that many city hotels cater for business people and charge higher rates in the week and lower at the weekend. The opposite can be said for country retreats which tend to have an influx of customers for the weekend and so offer better rates on weekdays. If you've got your heart set on a certain hotel but it's way out of your price range, why not compromise? Treat yourselves to some serious luxury for a couple of days at the end of your honeymoon.

First nights

No matter how long you've been together, the first night after your wedding is a very special one and you're going to want it to be as romantic as possible. If your reception has been held in a venue that has accommodation, you may want to stay there. Some couples don't like the idea of meeting mums and dads and Auntie Freda at a wedding breakfast the morning after the night before, and choose to stay somewhere away from their family on their wedding night. The groom traditionally books the hotel, but you may want to give him a gentle helping hand to ensure that it's perfect. The first-night venue should be near the reception, so you aren't travelling for hours to get there.

The type of hotel depends purely on your taste. If you're a city girl who hates the countryside, you're not going to want to stay in a manor house in the middle of rolling hills for the weekend. Check the hotel has a bridal suite, or a room that's extra special for you and your man to relax in. Romantic features like an extra-large bath tub for two, four-poster bed or balcony make all the difference. Let the hotel know that you're newly weds, and you may get a free room upgrade and extras like a bottle of champagne.

> ☺ Arrange for the best man to have your cases sent to the hotel, so that you won't be worrying about them during the day.

Weddings abroad

The idea of escaping to an exotic island to get married has never been so popular. More than 30,000 British couples a year now jet off to tie the knot and the number's growing each year. The attraction for lots of couples is that it is far more economical than a conventional wedding in the UK, which now costs an average of around £13,500. A wedding abroad on a paradise island like St Lucia in the Caribbean can cost from around £2000, and that includes the honeymoon!

A wedding abroad is also a good idea if you have family complications that are preventing you from going ahead with a formal wedding in the UK. It's also a popular choice with couples marrying the second time around.

If you want to marry abroad, the best place to head for some sound advice about where to go and how to do it is an experienced tour operator. Companies such as First Choice and Kuoni have dedicated wedding brochures with packages designed to make the whole experience hassle-free. They will be able to advise you as to the countries in which it is possible to arrange a civil or religious ceremony, what you need legally before you can tie the knot and prices for wedding packages. Budget-conscious couples could consider couples-only resorts such as Sandals, which offer free wedding packages if you book a certain number of nights in their resorts. Hotel wedding packages do tend to be rather basic, however, so you may want to discuss with a wedding co-ordinator at the destination any extras that you require, such as a musician or a videographer.

Sex talk

Whether you have been living together for a long time, or have not made love until your wedding night, here are a few tips for your first night and honeymoon.

- If you're both too tired on your wedding night to make love, don't panic or feel let down. It's a fact that a high percentage of couples are so exhausted by the end of the night that they can only just manage to drag themselves to bed, let alone get passionate. If this happens to you, make a pact to make up for it on your honeymoon. There's also nothing to stop you getting into the mood the morning after. Order a breakfast of strawberries and champagne (if your hangovers aren't too bad) on room service.

- If you've had to wear some body-sculpting underwear to fit into your wedding dress, which is more Bridget Jones big pants than Ann Summers saucy lingerie, then change out of it when you get to your first-night hotel and slip into something a bit more sultry. There's no need to go for suspender belt and stockings, but invest in something more sexy than you'd usually wear, particularly if you've been living together for a while – he'll be putty in your hands.
- If you're on the pill, be sure to take all you need to cover the amount of time you'll be away. If you don't want your period to occur while you're on holiday, it is possible to continue taking the pill without a break between packets to keep it at bay, but consult your GP first before you decide to do this.
- Unless you want to conceive during your honeymoon, it's wise to take a pack of condoms away with you, even if you're on the pill. You may fall ill during your trip, which can weaken the strength of the pill and expose you to the risk of pregnancy.

Medical advice

If you're honeymooning in an exotic destination you'll need to check well in advance if you need inoculations against diseases such as malaria, hepatitis B and C and typhoid. Visit your GP at least three months before the date you're due to fly off for advice about anything required for that destination. Some treatments involve a series of jabs over several weeks or medication that must be started sometime before you leave.

You don't want your honeymoon to be ruined by a stomach bug or travel sickness, so it's a good idea to prepare a small medical kit in case of any emergencies. Ideal things to pack include pills for diarrhoea and travel sickness, as well as headache tablets.

Packing it in

Tempting as it is to take away everything from your curling tongs to the kitchen sink when you jet off on your dream trip, you're going to have to be selective. Not only are there weight restrictions on planes, you also won't want to be lugging huge suitcases around with you on your honeymoon.

Those in the know, like cabin crew and pilots, save their backs and lots of time by taking a suitcase that can be pulled along on wheels. They then glide through airports with minimum fuss while everyone else is huffing and puffing their luggage up the escalators.

In terms of what to pack, the key is co-ordination. If you're going away for ten days or more, it's going to be easier if you can mix and match rather than try to take a different outfit for each day. If you put together a good combination of five skirts/trousers and five tops, you'll be able to switch them around and create ten fresh outfits.

You'll need to adjust your wardrobe to the country and climate to which you're travelling. If it's a hot climate with little chance of rain or cold, then you can get away with shorts and sun dresses. If there's a risk of showers, you'll need something waterproof and if it's going to be cold, you'll need lots of space for pullovers and jackets. Start planning at least two weeks before the big day. Lay out want you want to take away with you on your bed, and if there's something vital missing, like a cool bikini, you've got time to go and buy one.

Take a small range of versatile footwear such as flip flops, high-heeled sandals and trainers. It's a good idea to take a pair of socks and trainers even if you don't think you'll need them, as you may decide to go walking or riding once you get out there.

☺ Take two smart outfits for the evening, as many hotels ask guests to dress more formally for dinner.

Honeymoon luggage checklist

Luggage
- ❏ Coat or jacket
- ❏ Dress
- ❏ Lingerie
- ❏ Shoes
- ❏ Skirts
- ❏ Smart outfit
- ❏ Socks
- ❏ Sun hat
- ❏ Swim wear
- ❏ Tops
- ❏ Trainers
- ❏ Trousers

Hand luggage
- ❏ Book

- ❏ Camera and film
- ❏ Jewellery
- ❏ Passport
- ❏ Personal stereo
- ❏ Tickets

Toiletries
- ❏ 2-in-1 shampoo
- ❏ Deodorant
- ❏ Face wipes
- ❏ Make-up
- ❏ Medical kit
- ❏ Moisturiser
- ❏ Mosquito repellent
- ❏ Perfume
- ❏ Sunscreen SPF 15 plus

Honeymoon beauty

Hair

Don't neglect your hair if you're going on a honeymoon in the sun. It needs protecting just as much as your skin does. The best way to ensure that it doesn't go dry and brittle or change colour in the sun is to wear a hat. If you do have to expose your hair to the sun, buy a hair sunscreen that contains a UV filter. You can also buy after-sun products that will condition your hair and redress any damage caused by salt water and heat. If your hair tends to go frizzy in the heat, invest in a serum that will make it sleek and shiny whatever the weather.

Make-up

You will probably want a natural look to your honeymoon make-up. A sweep of mascara and a dab of lip gloss will do, but don't forget to pack a bronzer and brush to sweep over your cheeks, forehead and nose for that lovely sun-kissed look. Keeping your make-up to a minimum will also save space. If you are out in the sun, remember that your skin will get darker when it tans, so your usual foundation will be several shades too light. If you want to take a foundation buy one slightly darker than your usual shade or, better still, take a tinted moisturiser, which allows your natural glow to shine through.

Sunbathing babe

It's all too tempting to lie out in the sun as soon as you get to your destination. Not only is it likely that you'll burn if you do this, which means you'll find it painful to sunbathe for several days afterwards, it's also dangerous as it exposes you to the risk of skin cancer.

The simple rules to safe sunbathing are:

- Take it easy in the fist few days, and wear a sunscreen of SPF 15 plus.
- Always apply sunscreen before you go outside, not when you start sunbathing. This means that you won't leave your skin unprotected and are less likely to miss bits.
- Don't forget areas like the tops of ears, shoulders and feet, which burn easily.

- Try to stay in the shade at midday (12–2pm) when the sun is at its hottest. If you do go out during that time wear a hat to protect yourself from sun stroke.
- Keep drinking lots of water as your body will dehydrate in the sun.
- If you're going on boat trips or excursions, take a bottle of water and some sun block with you.

Cabin care

For your hand luggage, invest in a good-size bag that will comfortably hold all of your valuables, such as camera and jewellery. It's a good idea to take a few beauty items on board with you too as cabin air can be very dehydrating for the skin. Ask department-store beauty counters for miniature samples of moisturiser to take with you on your journey and invest in a good eye cream to help prevent dark circles and puffiness.

Avoid both dehydration and drowsiness on planes by drinking lots of water. Take your own bottle on board as attendants tend to give out small cupfuls. You may want to have a celebratory bottle of wine or glass of champagne when you board, but try not to carry on boozing as it will dehydrate you and hinder your recovery from jet lag.

If you find it hard to sleep on planes and you've got a very long flight, take a mask to cover your eyes and cut out all light, and ear plugs to block out noise. Aeroplane cabins can also get cold during long flights, so you may want to take a wrap or pashmina to cuddle up in.

Chapter 11
The Future

Embarking on your married life together is tremendously exciting but it can also be daunting. You are in the adventure of life together now and that can take some serious adjusting to. When the whirlwind of the wedding plans takes over your life there isn't much time to think about the future, but when it's over you may come down to earth with a bump.

What do we do when it's all over?
Some couples will sigh with relief that the hectic schedule has ceased, but it's all too common for brides to feel a bit empty or redundant when the wedding day has passed and life has got back to normal. If you've been planning a big event for six months or more, it's bound to have taken up a lot of your time and energy. When these are suddenly no longer needed, you can feel as if there is a bit of a hole in your life.

As well as throwing yourself into your new marriage, work and other activities, there are lots of marriage-related events that you can organise during the first year of married life. A romantic weekend away during the first six months is a good idea – you could plan it as a surprise. You could also plan a party for any friends or relatives who were unable to make it to the wedding, or to show people the wedding photos and video of the big day.

Anniversaries

There's your first wedding anniversary to think about. Why not make this into a special occasion to remember the wedding day?

Traditionally, each wedding anniversary is associated with a particular material, which would have been given as a wedding gift, such as paper products for the first year, and hard-wearing diamonds for the 60th anniversary.

For your second anniversary, which is cotton, you could give new clothes or, if you want something a little more fun, you could unwind a piece of cotton around the house, tie a gift at one end of it and give your partner the other end. If money is no object, how about planning a trip to The Cotton House Hotel in Mustique in the Caribbean?

Traditional anniversary gifts

- One year: paper
- Two years: cotton
- Three years: leather or straw
- Four years: silk or flowers
- Five years: wood
- Six years: iron or sugar
- Seven years: wool or copper
- Eight years: bronze
- Nine years: pottery
- Ten years: tin
- Eleven years: steel
- Twelve years: silk and fine linen

- Thirteen years: lace
- Fourteen years: ivory
- Fifteen years: crystal
- Twenty years: china
- Twenty-five years: silver
- Thirty years: pearl
- Thirty-five years: coral
- Forty years: ruby
- Forty-five years: sapphire
- Fifty years: gold
- Fifty-five years: emerald
- Sixty years: diamond

Chapter 12
Useful Contacts

H ere you should find all the important numbers and web sites you could ever need to plan your wedding to perfection. Please note that neither the author nor the publisher can directly recommend any of these companies by including them in this list. *All web site addresses are preceded by:* **www.**

Chapter 1 – Getting Started
Wedding organisers

Alternative Occasions	01932 872115	stressfreeday.com
Siobhan Craven-Robins	020 7481 4338	siobhancraven-robins.co.uk
Virgin Bride	020 7321 0866	virgin.com/bride
Cool White	020 7351 7899	coolwhite.com

Jewellers

H Samuel	0800 3894683	hsamuel.co.uk
Tiffany & Co	020 7409 2790	tiffany.com/uk
Garrard	020 7758 8520	garrard.com

Hen nights

Activity Superstore	01799 526526	activitysuperstore.com
Last Night of Freedom	08707 514433	lastnightoffreedom.co.uk
Party Bus	020 7233 0022	partybus.co.uk
Red Letter Days	020 8442 2001	redletterdays.co.uk

Chapter 2 – Budgeting
Insurance

Ecclesiastical Direct	0800 336622	ecclesiastical.co.uk
E&L Insurance Services	08707 423710	eandl.co.uk
Jackson Emms & Co	0118 957 5491	weddingsurance.co.uk

Chapter 3 – The Ceremony

Baptist Union	01235 517700	baptist.org.uk
British Humanist Ass.	020 7430 0908	humanism.org.uk
Catholic Marriage Care	020 7371 1341	marriagecare.org.uk
Church of England	020 7898 1000	cofe.anglican.org
Church of Scotland	0131 225 5722	churchofscotland.org.uk
General Register Office for England and Wales	0151 4714200	statistics.gov.uk
General Register Office for Northern Ireland	028 9025 2000	groni.gov.uk
General Register Office for Scotland	0131 314 4447	gro-scotland.gov.uk
Jewish Marriage Council	020 8203 6311	jmc-uk.org
Methodist Church	020 7222 8010	methodist.org.uk
United Reformed Church	020 7916 2020	urc.org.uk

Chapter 4 – Stationery

Adrienne Kerr Designs	0131 3325393	adriennekerrdesigns.co.uk
Belly Button Designs	0161 4489333	bellybuttondesigns.com
Comet & Cupid	07866 153387	
Conrad Design	0121 4283608	
Debenhams	020 7580 3000	debenhams.com

Diddy Gilly Designs	0161 643 8132	diddygilly.co.uk
Hayley Francesconi	01509 621118	
Jellyfish Designs	01939 233901	
Marks & Spencer	08706 080505	marksandspencer.com
Marlborough Calligraphy	01332 874420	marlbcall.com
Smythson of Bond Street	020 7629 8558	smythson.com
Tin Tickler Designs	01446 738600	
The Whole Caboodle	01803 813726	whole-caboodle.co.uk
WHSmith	01793 616161	whsmith.co.uk

Chapter 5 – Style and Beauty
Designer dresses

Alan Hannah	020 8882 0007	alanhannah.co.uk
Alfred Angelo	01908 262626	alfredangelo.co.uk
Amanda Wakeley	020 7471 8821	amandawakeley.com
Angela Vickers	0115 941 5616	angela-vickers.co.uk
Anna Christina Couture	020 8527 7001	annachristina.com
Basia Zarzyka	020 7730 1660	basias.com
Blue	029 2062 4477	bluebridalwear.co.uk
Caroline Holmes	020 7823 7678	carolineholmes.com
Catherine Walker	020 7581 8811	
Christiana Couture	020 7976 5252	christianacouture.com
David Fielden	020 7351 0067	
Donna Salado	01604 792869	donnasaladobridalwear.com
Eternity Bridal	01423 565444	eternitybridal.co.uk
Helen Marina	020 8361 3777	helenmarina.com
Ian Stuart International	01908 615599	ianstuart.com

Jasper Conran at		
The Wedding Shop	020 7838 0171	theweddingshoponline.com
Jessica McClintock	020 8909 2690	jessicamcclintock.com
Maggie Sottero	0151 355 6572	maggiesotterobridal.com
Margaret Lee	01702 616180	margaretlee.co.uk
Mori Lee	01476 591306	morileeinc.com
Neil Cunningham	020 7437 5793	neilcunningham.com
Peter Brandon Couture	01604 792849	peterbrandon.com
Phillipa Lepley	020 7386 0927	
Rena Koh	0906 110 0020	renakoh.uk.com
Ritva Westenius	020 7706 0708	ritvawestenius.co.uk
Ronald Joyce	020 7636 8989	ronaldjoyce.com
Sassi Holford	01823 256308	sassiholford.co.uk
Sharon Cunningham	020 7724 7002	sharoncunningham.com
Shelagh M	01978 661008	
Sophie English	020 7828 9007	sophie-english.co.uk
Suzanne Neville	020 8423 3161	suzanneneville.com
Vera Wang at		
The Wedding Shop	020 7838 0171	theweddingshoponline.com
Virgin Bride	020 7321 0866	virgin.com/bride

High-street dresses

Bhs	020 7262 3288	bhs.co.uk
Debenhams	020 7580 3000	debenhams.com
House of Fraser	020 7963 2000	houseoffraser.co.uk
Monsoon	020 7313 3000	monsoon.co.uk
Pronuptia	01273 563006	pronuptia.co.uk

Larger-size dresses

Alfred Angelo	01908 262626	alfredangelo.co.uk
Berkertex Bride	01476 593311	bbride.com
Eternity Bridal	01423 565444	eternitybridal.co.uk
Ian Stuart International	01908 615599	ianstuart.com
Papillon	020 8345 6725	weddings.co.uk/papillon
Sincerity	01908 615511	sinceritybridal.com
Sallie Bee	0121 708 1841	sposabella.co.uk

Bridesmaids' dresses

Alan Hannah	020 8882 0007	alanhannah.co.uk
Berkertex Bride	020 7287 7090	bbride.com
Bhs	020 7262 3288	bhs.co.uk
Jessica McClintock	020 8908 2690	jessicamcclintock.com
Jim Hjelm Occasions	0800 328 1531	jimhjelmvisions.com
LouLou	01322 440225	wloulou.co.uk
Monsoon	020 7313 3000	monsoon.co.uk
Olive	01460 66110	olivebridal.com
Pretty Maids	0116 2549636	
Ronald Joyce	020 7636 8989	ronaldjoyce.com
Virgin Bride	020 7321 0866	virgin.com/bride

Accessories

Blossom Tiaras	01252 851733	blossom.co.uk
Carousel	0115 9110466	carouselveils.com
Halo & Co	01283 704305	haloandco.com
Johnny Loves Rosie	020 7247 1496	johnnylovesrosie.co.uk
Joyce Jackson Veils	01745 343689	joycejacksonveils.com

Palmer Design		
Headdresses	01604 686384	
Tiaraworks	01903 782472	

Shoes

Diane Hassall	01832 730066	pureandprecious.com
HKE	01323 728 988	henrykaye.co.uk
Jimmy Choo	020 7591 7000	jimmychoo.com
Rainbow Club	01392 207030	rainbowclub.co.uk
Shades Shoes	0113 243 8067	shadesshoes.com

Chapter 6 – Flowers
Florists

April Flowers	0115 977 1358	aprilflowersnottingham.co.uk
The Flowers & Plants		
Association	020 7738 8044	flowers.org.uk
Jane Packer	020 7935 2673	janepacker.com
Kenneth Turner	020 7355 3880	
Mary Jane Vaughan		
at Fast Flowers	020 7385 8400	
Paula Pryke	020 7837 7336	paula-pryke-flowers.com
Tiger Rose	01730 829989	tiger-rose.co.uk

Chapter 7 – Photography
Photographers

British Institute of		
Professional		
Photography	01920 464011	bipp.com

Guild of Wedding Photographers	01225 760088	guildofphotographers.com
Master Photographers Association	01325 356555	mpauk.com
Society of Wedding & Portrait Photographers	01745 815030	swpp.co.uk

Videographers

Association of Professional Videomakers	01529 4217171	pineappleuk.com/apv
Institute of Videography	0845 741 3626	iov.co.uk
Yourcast TV	020 7586 1441	yourcast.tv

Chapter 8 – The Reception
Cakes

Cakes For All	01623 871375	geocities.com/cakesforall
Choccywoccydoodah	020 7724 5465	choccywoccydoodah.com
Fantasy Wedding Cakes	01295 254556	
Helen Houlden	0115 933 3751	helenhouldencakes.co.uk
The Icing Centre	01934 624565	
Jane Asher Party Cakes	020 7584 6177	jane-asher.co.uk
Pat-A-Cake Pat-A-Cake	020 7485 0006	
Purita Hyam	01403 891518	
Rachel Mount	020 8672 9333	
Tracey's Cakes	01844 347147	traceyscakes.co.uk

Catering/Hire

First Quench	01707 387200	firstquench.co.uk
Top Table Hire	01327 260575	toptablehire.com
WA Carr & Son Ltd	01923 773611	

Crèche services
The Wedding Crèche

Service	01483 202490	weddingcreche.com

Favours

BB Favours	01832 275191	
Belle Bomboniere	0121 421 3182	bellebomboniere.co.uk
Chocolate Chatter	01952 884511	chocolatechatter.co.uk
La Bomboniera	020 7437 2916	labomboniera.co.uk
The Very Nice Company	01884 232152	theverynicecompany.com
The White House	01905 381149	the-whitehouse.uk.com

Music
Central England

Music Agency	0870 702 3456	musiciansofnote.co.uk
Wedding Solutions	0870 755 0369	foxevents365.com

Chapter 9 – Gifts

Argos	0870 600 2525	argos.co.uk
Bliss	01428 681945	blissonline.com
British Airways		
Travel Shops	0870 240 0747	batravelshops.com
Confetti	0870 840 6060	confetti.co.uk

Debenhams	020 7580 3000	debenhams.com
Fenwick	020 8202 8200	fenwick.co.uk
House of Fraser	020 7963 2236	houseoffraser.co.uk
John Lewis	020 7629 7711	johnlewis.com
Thomas Cook Wedding List Service	0870 750 2222	thomascookweddinglist.co.uk
Wedding List Services	020 7978 1118	wedding.co.uk
The Wedding Present Company	01926 411455	weddingpresentlists.co.uk

Chapter 10 – The Honeymoon

Abercrombie & Kent	0845 070 0620	abercrombiekent.co.uk
Airtours Weddings	0870 241 2568	
Cosmos	0870 264 6020	cosmos-holidays.co.uk
First Choice	0870 750 0465	firstchoice.co.uk
Kuoni Travel	01306 747007	kuoni.co.uk/weddings
Sandals Resorts	020 7590 0212	sandals.co.uk
Tradewinds	0870 751 0009	tradewinds.co.uk
Tropical Places	01342 330753	tropicalplaces.co.uk

Index

Other wedding books from Foulsham